HISTORY'S
NAUGHTY
BITS

HISTORY'S
NAUGHTY
BITS

KAREN
DOLBY

METRO BOOKS
New York

METRO BOOKS
New York

An Imprint of Sterling Publishing
387 Park Avenue South
New York, NY 10016

Cover design by Ana Bježančević
Designed and typeset by www.glensaville.com

ISBN 978-1-4351-5424-7

For information about custom editions, special sales, and premium
and corporate purchases, please contact Sterling Special Sales at
800-805-5489 or specialsales@sterlingpublishing.com.

Printed and bound by CPI Group (UK) Ltd, Croydon, CR0 4YY

2   4   6   8   10   9   7   5   3   1

www.sterlingpublishing.com

CONTENTS

INTRODUCTION

Philip Larkin in his poem 'Annus Mirabilis' contributed some of the most witty lines to sum up the sexual revolution.

Was he right? Did sexual liberation really begin in the 1960s with free love, the introduction of the Pill and that potent mix of sex and drugs and rock 'n' roll? Or was it during the 1950s, when the widespread use of penicillin reduced the dangers of infection from 'risky behaviour', which was coincidentally or otherwise accompanied by a spike in levels of illegitimate births and cases of gonorrhoea?

But what about the freedom from convention offered by the Second World War – a loosening of morals because, quite frankly, what was the point when everyone could be dead tomorrow? And then there was the First World War and the international flu pandemic of 1918, whose lucky survivors ushered in an era of bright young things in which 'anything goes'.

Or look further back. Were things really so different in earlier decades, or even millennia? Eighteenth-century archaeologists excavating the ancient Roman cities of Pompeii and Herculaneum could barely move for phallic art and erotic frescoes. Delve just a little deeper into history's seamier side and it turns out we've always been obsessed with sex. Kingdoms have been won and lost because of it, fortunes made and reputations ruined.

If you remain in any doubt as to the age-old obsession with sex, let's go back further still. Forty thousand years ago, when Prehistoric man was struggling to survive the Ice Age, living in caves and waging a constant battle against lack of food and attacks by wild animals, he still had the inclination to sculpt Venus figurines – hundreds of which survive – endowed with pendulous breasts and exaggerated buttocks. Made for holding rather than displaying, the figurines appear to have no practical purpose other than giving pleasure. Every generation thinks of its predecessors as old-fashioned, prim, proper, inhibited and even boring. It's simply not true. From the first pornographer to the first reported case of auto-erotic asphyxiation, beginning with the Ancient World and continuing with the saints – and, of course, sinners – of the Middle Ages, through the poets and bawds of the Renaissance, the misadventures of royalty, and the thriving underworld of the Georgians and Victorians, *History's Naughty Bits* looks at what was really going on – both behind closed doors and for all the world to see.

As the twelfth-century monk and chronicler Richard of Devizes wrote, 'Actors, jesters, smooth-skinned lads, Moors, flatterers, pretty boys, effeminates, pederasts, singing and dancing girls, quacks, belly-dancers, sorceresses, extortioners, night-wanderers, magicians, mimes, beggars, buffoons: all this tribe fill all the houses.' They have done since time immemorial and will continue to do as long as men and women have a pulse.

A CLASSICAL EDUCATION

Give me a thousand kisses, then a hundred, then another thousand. Catullus

Classical writers may not have invented sex but they were among the first to document it in graphic detail. As the royal philosopher King Solomon, writing in Ecclesiastes nearly 3,000 years ago, commented, 'There is nothing new under the sun.' And it's a theory that certainly seems to have been borne out by the Ancient Greeks and Romans: however perverse the practice, they almost always tried it first. It is no coincidence that many modern words connected with sex, from aphrodisiac and eroticism to nymphomania and zoophilia, are Greek in origin …

IT'S A MAN'S WORLD

Classical Greece was a great place to be a man and less so to be a woman – or at least a respectable woman, who was expected to remain chaste and be rarely seen. Married women usually stayed at home with other women while their husbands socialized. Wives rarely dined with their husbands and never if there were guests.

Women were generally not regarded highly by the ancient Greeks and they had few legal or political rights. You only have to look at their flawed goddesses and positively malevolent fictional heroines: Euripides' vengeful Medea, who murdered her cut up her brother, is just one case in point. For many men, the only point in marrying was to have legitimate heirs, so it is little wonder that women wanting to be relatively free might be drawn to the life of a courtesan. Known as *hetairai*, high-class courtesans were usually well educated and respected, holding positions in society reminiscent of later European royal mistresses. In the fourth century BC, the Athenian statesman and orator Demosthenes wrote, 'We have *hetairai* for our pleasure, concubines for our daily needs, and wives to give us legitimate children and look after the housekeeping.'

NOT TONIGHT, DARLING

The lack of social relationship between married couples had an effect on the birth rate, and large families were virtually unknown. The historian and philosopher Xenophon evidently saw this as a grave problem in the third century BC, decreeing that, 'by law, a couple lacking a legitimate heir is required to have sex at least three times a month' until the wife became pregnant.

One sinister result of the low status of women was a high level of female infanticide, with baby girls abandoned or left to their fate outside on open hillsides. Over in Sparta, male infanticide was also practised if the baby was considered too weak or imperfect in some way: a brutal early form of eugenics.

MALE WORKOUTS

Wrestlers on an ancient Greek vase painting

At its extreme, the modern stereotype of Classical Greece is of open homosexuality, appreciation of the male form culminating in naked wrestling, and mixed public baths where anything was permissible. The reality was rather different – both more innocent and more shocking.

On the one hand, the public baths were strictly segregated, male and female, and never mixed. On the other, Greek gymnasiums were all-male preserves where the athletes did indeed wrestle in the nude.

The word gymnasium comes from *gymnos*, meaning 'naked'.

But gymnasiums were designed to train young men not just to wrestle but also to exercise and compete in a variety of sports in preparation for public games. They were also meeting places, where philosophical and intellectual debate might take place.

Exercise was viewed as an important part of a young man's education, stressing as it did health and strength. Athletes were naked as a tribute to the gods and also to encourage an aesthetic appreciation of the male form. One can see how this might be open to different interpretation.

MENTORING

Similarly, it was customary for well-educated men to 'adopt' teenage males, acting as intellectual guides to complete the youths' moral and social development when their formal schooling ended. 'Since we are all likely to go astray,' Sophocles once said, 'the reasonable thing is to learn from those who can teach.'

Classical scholars disagree as to whether any physical relationship was traditionally involved in these educational mentorships, but the fact that philosophers including Socrates, Plato and Aristotle felt compelled to condemn homosexuality with adolescents suggests that relations were not always entirely innocent. That said, and education aside, homosexuality between adult and teenage males was certainly not entirely taboo in Ancient Greece, as vase paintings often rather graphically show. By the fifth century BC the practice of *paiderastia*, or pederasty, was well established in Greek culture.

THE MORAL BROTHEL

Solon, the Athenian statesman and lawmaker, horrified by the economic and moral decline he identified in Athens in the sixth century BC, attempted to provide a solution by setting up state-run brothels.

Adultery was considered less of a sin if it was committed with a prostitute rather than with another citizen's wife. Foreign slaves, both male and female, were brought in from across the empire and prices were fixed helpfully low so that anyone could afford them. An added bonus was that the brothels paid taxes, which was good for the city coffers, too.

At one such brothel archaeologists have uncovered a pair of sandals with 'Follow Me' embossed on the soles, to leave an enticing imprint on the ground.

TRUST ME, I'M A DOCTOR

Hippocrates is referred to as the father of Western medicine and doctors today still take the Hippocratic Oath – a promise to practise medicine honestly – which is based on some of the principles he put forward. Working at the beginning of the fourth century BC, Hippocrates revolutionized medicine and developed a number of interesting scientific theories.

His ideas on orgasm, however, were rather one-sided in favour of men. In common with other doctors of the period, he believed women produced female semen. He also thought that women's pleasure during sex only peaked when the man ejaculated. He held another theory that a male child (obviously preferable) would be conceived if a man reached orgasm first, while if the woman climaxed before the man the baby would unfortunately be a girl.

THE FEMININE TOUCH

It was perhaps not surprising that Greek wives were left feeling frustrated and undersexed. Some engaged the services of a procuress to find a lover, but the punishment if caught was severe and there were, after all, other less risky options. Masturbation was regarded as a healthy outlet rather than a hidden vice and there are records of dildos made from wood or padded leather, which had to be well soaked with olive oil before use.

Women also turned to each other. The Greeks called lesbians *tribas*, derived from the verb for 'to rub', although the word homosexual could apply to men or women, deriving from *homos*, meaning the same, rather than from the Latin *homo*, man. It was only in the nineteenth century that the word lesbian evolved from Lesbos, the island home of the Greek poet Sappho, who famously wrote poems about women in the sixth century BC.

BEAUTIFUL BUTTOCKS

An ancient Greek dancer

Ancient Greek attitudes towards women changed over time. Art and literature began to reflect romantic love between men and women and there was a greater appreciation of the female form in vase painting and statuary. There was particular preference for *callipygian* women, or those with beautiful buttocks, and women would sometimes even pad their posterior to appear more shapely.

TITILLATING TALES

One can't help but wonder if the stories were exaggerated to shock and thrill readers who then, as now, had a taste for such gossip, but if the ancient writers are anything to go by, the Greeks took a prurient interest in the sex lives of their neighbours.

Herodotus, author of the *Histories* in the fifth century BC, was also an explorer, traveller and storyteller. He wrote vivid accounts of the wonders he saw, the places he visited and the strange customs he witnessed. Among them, he commented on the Egyptian practice of keeping the bodies of beautiful women for a few days after death, until they began to decay. This was to discourage necrophilia, which was apparently not uncommon amongst embalmers at the time. He reported on ritual bestiality in Egypt and the insatiable sexual appetites of the Massagatae tribe, who lived near the Caspian Sea. The men of this people were said to have one wife each, yet the wives were 'held in common', suggesting they may have been shared among the men as sexual objects. There were also the weird customs of the Babylonians, who fumigated their genitals after sex and whose women would have intercourse with complete strangers once in their lives, at the temple of Mylitta (whom Herodotus indentified with Aphrodite), as an offering to the goddess.

WHEN IN ROME

Roman women had a little more freedom than their Greek counterparts. Certainly wealthier women enjoyed a degree of emancipation; they were allowed to divorce and retain some of their own property, and attended banquets and freely socialized with men. However, there was a definite divide between women as wives and women as whores.

Lucretius, a Roman poet and philosopher of the first century BC, wrote in his epic *On the Nature of the Universe* that the best position for conception was to approach the woman from behind with 'her loins uplifted high'. He asserted it was completely unnecessary for the wife to move at all; indeed he believed that movement interfered with conception and that it was to prevent conception that prostitutes writhed about. Besides, enjoyment wasn't regarded as part of the package for married women. According to St Jerome, Lucretius went mad after drinking a love potion and committed suicide.

Lucretius, framed by a laurel wreath

ONE RULE FOR MEN ...

Medea contemplating the death of her children to punish her
unfaithful husband Jason

Adultery was strictly forbidden for women but not for men –
other men's wives and virgin daughters were out of the question
but prostitutes and slaves were fair game. In the early years of
the Roman empire, adultery by women was punishable by death,
although this was later reduced to banishment and confiscation
of a third of her property – and husbands were not allowed
to forgive their erring wives either, or they would themselves
be punished..

The exception to the adultery rule seems to have led to a rush
of married women registering as prostitutes to get round the
strict laws.

THE EMPRESS'S BROTHEL

Tacitus, Suetonius and Pliny the Elder, along with other eminent writers, all recounted tales of the Empress Valeria Messalina, wife of the Emperor Claudius, who ran a brothel, where she worked as a prostitute under a false name. There she organized orgies for other wealthy Roman women, competing in all-night sex competitions with other prostitutes, which she usually won with up to twenty-five different partners. It was claimed she used sex to increase her own power and to control politicians. Messalina also manipulated Claudius into agreeing to the exile or execution of anyone she considered a threat to her position. Claudius later had her executed.

Messalina may have been an extreme example, but enough women must have registered as prostitutes to raise concern. In AD 19 the Senate, supported by the Emperor Tiberius, ruled that no descendant of or anyone married to a Roman knight was allowed to work as a prostitute.

MORAL PERVERSITY

There were three types of marriage in ancient Rome. Two of them involved ceremonies of varying levels of complexity while the third, which became increasingly popular, simply entailed living together continuously for a year, any break meaning the year had to begin again. Divorce also became easier. Adultery was the most obvious reason, but moral laxity, drunkenness and infertility were all considered reasonable grounds for divorce.

Julius Caesar's adopted son and successor, the Emperor Augustus, divorced his wife Scribonia for 'moral perversity', which in reality meant she disliked and disapproved of his new seventeen-year-old mistress, Livia Drusilla, who was six months pregnant with her own husband's child.

Upper-class Roman families sometimes forced couples to divorce for political or dynastic reasons. Augustus's daughter Julia, for example, was pressured into divorcing her husband in order to marry Tiberius, who himself had been persuaded to divorce his beloved wife Vipsania – who also happened to be Julia's stepdaughter.

HAIR AND MAKE-UP

Beauty routines were fairly elaborate in Ancient Rome. Although women's clothes were not as revealing as those of the Greeks, the emphasis was on full make-up, starting with face packs and foundation and moving on to kohl eyeliner, eye shadow and red dye pastes to colour cheeks and lips. Classical women may have been dab hands with a make-up brush but waterproof products had yet to be developed: in the heat of a Roman summer, or in the rain, make-up melted, leaving clown-like trails of red and black down many a woman's cheeks.

Hair was crimped and curled into ringlets. There appears to

have been the same horror of grey hair and signs of ageing that people feel today, and similar attempts to hide it. Grey hairs were dyed or removed with tweezers. There was a particular vogue for red-blonde hair, like that of the Goth and Saxon tribes of Germany, while other dyes included a bizarre list of ingredients, from scorpions and birds' heads mixed with laudanum or opium to ox gall. Expensive wigs were another option, made with hair from distant India.

After make-up and hair, perfumed oils and jewellery were liberally applied to complete an alluring feminine aura. Perhaps it is little wonder that Roman men had roving eyes.

A WINNING SMILE

Tooth-whitening is not a modern phenomenon: in a bid to look younger and more attractive, the Romans used an enticing mixture of goats' milk and urine to whiten their teeth.

ROMAN BATHS

As classical statues suggest, the Roman fashion was for fully shaved pubic hair and general depilation for women, but also to some extent for men. It was generally seen as hygienic and neater to be trimmed, but gay men took this shaving further as an obvious signal to others. And the baths gave plenty of opportunity for Roman men to get the measure of one another.

The poet Martial, best known for his witty epigrams satirizing Roman life, made several blatant comments about men's assets, including: 'Your penis and your nose are so large, Papylua, that you can smell it whenever you have an erection.' He also asked the Roman general Labienus: 'You pluck the hair from your chest, legs and arms; and your shaven penis is surrounded by short hair; you do this for your mistress's sake, we know. But, Labienus, for whom do you depilate your arsehole?'

As in Ancient Greece, it was not unknown for wealthy men to have younger male companions and the exploits of more than one emperor encouraged a certain amount of sexual liberalism.

ALL IS VANITY

Julius Caesar: soldier, statesman, author, leader of Rome, conqueror of Britain and Gaul, instigator of an extensive programme of social and political reforms, creator of the Julian Calendar, and eventually 'Dictator in Perpetuity' – until his assassination on the Ides of March in 44 BC, of course. He is regarded as one of the greatest military commanders of all time and the list of his achievements is impressive, to say the least. And yet he was not without his insecurities.

Busts of Caesar's head and distinct close-cropped hairstyle are instantly recognizable today, but in reality he was sensitive about his receding hairline. He kept his hair well groomed to compensate for this, wearing a laurel wreath whenever possible as a useful disguise. He regularly shaved his beard but is also reported to have plucked excess facial hair and other undesirable body hair.

In Caesar's day, it was common for centurions to have pierced nipples to show their virility and loyalty to Rome. As a sign of strength and solidarity with his army, Caesar's nipples were likewise pierced.

According to Cicero, Plutarch and Suetonius, among others, as well as the bawdy songs of his soldiers, Caesar was an insatiable lover. He was married three times and had numerous affairs, including with Cleopatra, with whom he had a son, Caesarion. Despite his rampant heterosexual reputation, rumours of a homosexual affair that had occurred in around 80 BC, when Caesar was a young man of twenty, taunted him throughout his life. He had been sent to fetch a fleet from King Nicomedes IV of Bithynia, whom Rome was supporting against Mithridates of Pontus. Caesar stayed at Nicomedes' court longer than seemed necessary, however, and stories that he had shared the king's bed began to circulate. Years later joking references to Caesar as 'the Queen of Bithynia' were still being made, and the line 'enamoured of a king' was included in one of his soldier's songs.

Whatever the truth, Memmius and Cicero evidently believed the rumours at the time, and the story was later repeated by the historian Suetonius.

VESTAL VIRGINS

For Vestal Virgins the punishment for violating the oath of
celibacy was to be buried alive

Six Vestals were chosen to attend Vesta, goddess of the home, and
to guard the sacred fire. They were picked by lot from a shortlist
drawn up from the daughters of noble Roman families. Girls
were enrolled between the ages of six and ten and would serve
for thirty years, during which time they had to remain chaste.
Any hint that they were not resulted in a slow death, sealed in an
underground chamber.

The role was taken seriously: Vesta was said to control the
fate and prosperity of Rome. Whenever there was a vacancy,
many families tried to keep their daughters' names from the list,
possibly mostly out of concern for her wealth and property, which
would pass automatically to the state.

CRUDELY POETIC

The worship of Priapus

However sophisticated the Romans might have been, their humour seems to have been graphically rude and earthy.

Priapus was a minor Greek god of fertility, distinguished by his ridiculously oversized erection. Statues of the god became popular in Roman gardens, to scare away would-be thieves. They were often hung with crudely humorous warnings, which have been collected together in an anthology of poems called the *Priapeia*. For instance: 'I warn you, boy, you will be screwed; girl, you will be fucked; a third penalty awaits the bearded thief.' Even the poet Martial contributed: 'If your thieving rod harms the smallest shoots of this here vine, like it or not, this cypress rod will penetrate and plant a fig in you.'

Paintings of Priapus also survive; the best-known are from the House of the Vettii in Pompeii and a bar in Herculaneum, where it was considered a symbol of good luck for the customers.

Further brutally explicit verse comes from the quill of Catullus, who is normally better known for his sublime love poetry than for his seamier side. One of his poems was even considered too outrageous for the BBC to translate in 2009, when it became the focus of a sex discrimination court case in which an employer had supposedly quoted it in a text message.

The poem in question was XVI, written because Aurelius, 'you cocksucker', and Furius, 'you sodomite', had apparently called Catullus a sissy. It ends:

> *Because you've read of my x thousand*
> *Kisses you doubt my virility?*
> *I'll bugger you and stuff your gobs.*

This was not the first time that Aurelius had been the subject of Catullus's rather cheerfully obscene insults:

> *It's you I'm scared of and your penis,*
> *That menace to good boys and bad.*

In another poem Catullus refers to Aurelius and Furius as his comrades.

BACCHANALIAN CRIMES

Bacchus and Ariadne by Titian

As well as Priapus, the Romans also adopted the Greek god Dionysius, who they merged with their own fertility god, Liber, to become Bacchus.

At first the cult of Bacchus was celebrated as a three-day festival for women, held during daylight hours once a year, but it evolved into a full-scale celebration that was open to all, at night, five times a month. Flaming torches lit the orgiastic initiation rituals for young men and women and the event soon became an excuse for drunken debauchery, with frenzied music and dancing until dawn on the banks of the River Tiber. Out of control, with terrifying ordeals including flogging and even ritualized hanging, the Bacchic rites could easily conceal other premeditated crimes and even murder.

It was a plot to defraud and then murder a young man named Aebutius that brought the cult to the attention of the authorities. Having squandered Aebutius' property, his stepfather planned to conceal that crime by murdering the young man under cover of the Bacchanalian celebrations. His mother joined the conspiracy, persuading her son to go along to the rites as an initiate. Fortunately for Aebutius, his mistress Hispala Faecenia, a courtesan and intelligent woman of the world, was suspicious. The affair was reported and an investigation and prosecutions followed.

The historian Livy reported that 7,000 people were arrested in the Bacchic scandal. Some men were executed, others imprisoned, while women were generally treated more leniently and handed over to the custody of their relatives. In 186 BC the Senate ruled to restrict the cult to small licensed meetings in Rome and tried to ban it throughout the rest of the empire.

The cult of Bacchus was revived in a milder form in Julius Caesar's time, when it was celebrated as a carnival street procession, Mark Antony was said to be an enthusiast.

GO AND BE FRUITFUL

With so much illicit coupling going on, avoiding pregnancy became something of a fixation for the Romans. While they had a relatively detailed knowledge of human physiology, some of their ideas on contraception were fairly imaginative.

Soranus, an eminent physician, recommended either abstinence during the fertile days of the month or anal sex; failing that, wool plugs soaked in honey, oil and resin, or astringent solutions. Dioscorides favoured the use of black pepper. Sneezing followed by douching was generally approved.

Usually so sensible and measured, Pliny the Elder's answer was to reduce desire. Mouse dung, snail or pigeon excrement, and blood from ticks found on wild black bulls applied as an ointment, were among his suggestions. One can see such treatments being rather successful, though not quite in the way Pliny intended.

Far from needing contraception, the Romans were obsessed with their falling birth rate and the diminishing population. As in Ancient Greece, large families were uncommon. A high infant mortality rate was partly to blame, but the copious amounts of alcohol consumed, along with the lead absorbed from pipes and cooking pots, plus daily visits to the hot baths, probably all contributed to a reduction in fertility.

The Emperor Augustus tried to help the situation by ruling that widows must remarry within two years and divorcees within eighteen months. Property and inheritance laws were also changed to encourage marriage, financial rewards were offered to couples who had three living children, and rules against intermarriage between classes were relaxed. But all to no avail: the Roman population continued to fall.

POWER PLAY

I wish it, I command it. Let my will take the place of a reason. Juvenal

At its worst, Ancient Rome can seem to epitomize the old adage 'power corrupts'. Many wealthy Romans had the power to do whatever they wanted to whomever, and took full advantage of the fact.

Plutarch wrote about Lucius Quintus, a Roman senator, who had a prisoner beheaded at a dinner party for the amusement of his young lover. This was to make up for the fact that the young man had missed the execution at his first gladiatorial show because he had rushed away to meet Lucius. Dinner-party beheadings were obviously not considered acceptable behaviour, however, as Lucius Quintus was expelled from the Senate.

One of the most outrageous stories concerned Vedius Pollio, who fed slaves at will to the lamprey eels in his fishpond if they displeased him. This was deemed shockingly cruel, even by Roman standards, and Emperor Augustus himself intervened on behalf of a slave. One evening, when Augustus was dining with Vedius Pollio, a slave broke a crystal cup. To save the terrified servant, Augustus proceeded to smash all the crystal cups at the table.

> When Augustus inherited Vedius's magnificent villa on his death, he had it demolished so that the house would not remain as a monument to its evil owner.

'WHO WILL GUARD THE GUARDS?'

Many emperors ruled wisely, but for others their elevated position led to total degeneracy – often to the point of madness.

Tiberius's minnows

The Emperor Tiberius was dark and reclusive by nature, described by Pliny the Elder as 'the gloomiest of men'. Persuaded to divorce Vipsania, the woman he loved, he was unhappily married to Augustus's daughter Julia, by all accounts a promiscuous and manipulative character.

Tiberius would probably have been happier living the relatively quiet life of a Roman general and then retiring to obscurity. Instead he allowed himself to be persuaded by power and was miserable. The death of his son seems to have been the final straw and he lived the latter part of his life in semi-retirement on the isle of Capri.

There, he had a group of young boys he called his minnows trained to swim with him underwater, nibbling at his genitals as if they were fish. Male and female slaves from across the empire were dressed as nymphs and satyrs hidden in grottoes and glades in the woods, ready to pleasure him in any way he chose. Suetonius recorded Tiberius's fondness for threesomes and pornography, and his expectation that anyone who caught his roving eye would willingly comply.

During his rule, Tiberius consolidated the empire, leaving it considerably stronger and wealthier than he had found it. Sadly for him, history tends to focus on the more negative aspects of his personal life and his perverse predilections.

Tacitus reported that there was mass rejoicing at the news of Tiberius's death. He died at the age of seventy-seven in AD 37, probably of natural causes, although there were rumours that he had been smothered by Caligula, his heir, together with the praetorian prefect, Macro.

An insane tyrant

Tiberius was succeeded by his great-nephew and adopted grandson, Caligula, who appears to have begun his rule quietly enough but at some point lost all sense of moderation or morality, going on to become the archetype of a cruel tyrant.

One of the few surviving sources of information regarding Caligula's rule is Suetonius' *Twelve Caesars*, which often gives very sensationalized accounts, but nonetheless it is clear that Caligula had soon spent Tiberius's fortune and begun working to increase his unrestricted power as emperor. He appears to have had no redeeming qualities, on top of which he was physically unattractive. Seneca described him as tall, pale and thin, with sunken eyes and a weak chin, balding but otherwise hairy. He suffered from a condition that made him fall unconscious without warning and was an insomniac, plagued with strange delusions when he did sleep.

Various stories gave rise to reports of Caligula's insanity. He planned to have his favourite horse, Incitatus, appointed to a seat on the Senate, replaced the heads of public statues with his own, and when planning an expedition against Britain got no further than the Channel, where he inexplicably ordered his troops to collect seashells. And ensuring his position as the cruel despot by whom all others are judged, he tortured slaves, handed out the death penalty at random (woe betide anyone who looked down on his bald head) and was said to have thrown spectators to the lions when there were not enough convicts.

According to Suetonius, Caligula regularly committed incest with his three sisters, openly living with one of them, Drusilla, as if she were his wife, even though she was already married to a former consul. He was so grief-stricken at Drusilla's death that he made any sign of happiness a capital offence during the period of public mourning, including going to the baths or dining with family. Later he swore by her divinity when making public oaths.

Openly bisexual, it amused Caligula to examine the wives of his dinner guests and to select whoever took his fancy, later rating their sexual performance. It is perhaps not surprising that he was murdered by friends at the age of twenty-nine, having ruled for just under four years.

Arguably, Caligula's precedent began the chain of events that would lead to the fall of the ruling Julio-Claudian dynasty in AD 68.

While Rome burned

Nero was the last of the Julio-Claudian emperors and he seems to have continued where Caligula left off. A cruel tyrant, he was responsible for countless executions and poisonings, including the murder of his mother, Agrippina, and his stepbrother Britannicus. He ruled for fourteen years and was emperor in AD 64 when much of Rome was destroyed by fire. Indeed, many Romans believed Nero had started the blaze himself in order to clear land for his vast palace. The story of him playing the fiddle and singing 'The Fall of Troy' while the city burned below him is an enduring image, though probably not true.

Like many of his forebears, Nero was said to have perverse sexual tastes: Suetonius described him dressed in wild animal skins, attacking and clawing at the genitals of prisoners bound to stakes. The historian also claimed Nero was obsessed with his mother. Most extreme was his marriage in AD 67 to a young freedman named Sporus, whom he first ordered to be castrated. Sporus bore a remarkable resemblance to Nero's wife, Poppaea Sabina, who had died two years earlier. So grief-stricken was Nero at her death that he refused to allow her to be cremated.

Instead, her body was embalmed and placed in the Mausoleum of Augustus.

Nero committed suicide in AD 68, when he discovered that the Senate had sent soldiers to kill him.

Nero and Agrippina

BEDS, BAWDS
AND BARDS

Grant me chastity and self-control – but not yet.
St Augustine (before his conversion)

With the Middle Ages came restraint and rules. If sex had been fairly unbridled in the classical period, where almost anything goes, it was the medieval age when sex became dirty. St Augustine was partly to blame. After a hedonistic and permissive youth, he converted to Christianity in AD 387, going on to become one of the Church Fathers, who were influential theologians. His writings influenced the future of Western Christianity and philosophy, among other things, developing the concept of original sin. His strict rules set the tone. Laid down at the end of one great era, they held sway at the dawn of the next. People discovered guilt, and how to revel in it.

St Augustine's basic view was that sex was acceptable only within marriage and then only for procreation and if it was not enjoyed too much. There was to be no masturbation, oral or anal sex, no foreplay and no position other than missionary. The fact that so many different clerics felt it necessary to outline what was and was not a sin, together with the extensive and frankly bizarre lists of practices to avoid, suggests few people stuck to the rules – or the writers had wild imaginations. If pleasure was a sin, then the majority were sinners.

A NECESSARY EVIL

In reality, the medieval Church was more pragmatic in its approach and often turned a blind eye to what was really going on. In line with this, although prostitution was a punishable offence, it was also tolerated as a necessary evil.

St Augustine had said, 'Remove prostitutes from society and you will pollute all things with lust.' St Thomas Aquinas believed this too, making the analogy: 'Take away the sewer and you will fill the palace with pollution . . . Take away prostitutes from the world and you will fill it with sodomy.' (At the time sodomy was taken to mean any form of anal sex, bestiality, or general debauchery.)

There was a general fear, that without prostitutes, 'respectable' wives and daughters would be at risk. In thirteenth-century France, when pious King Louis IX tried to eradicate the brothels, there was a public outcry that the streets of Paris were no longer safe. And in Venice, courtesans were said to make up almost 4 per cent of the population.

In the Church's list of sexual offences, prostitution ranked as less of a sin than adultery, incest or homosexuality; birth control was also arguably worse. It was felt that women were not wholly culpable as they were easily tempted but as the story of Mary Magdalene demonstrated, they could also be redeemed.

LONDON'S STEWS

In England, acceptance of the inevitability of prostitution by the Church was the first step towards acceptance by the state. There were a number of private brothels and bath houses, something like the old Roman ones, which were known colloquially as 'stews'. In 1161, King Henry II passed his Ordinance for the Government of the Stewholders in Southwark, which effectively established a red-light district and left the brothels under the authority of the Bishop of Winchester for the next four centuries.

The regulated stewhouses were to be inspected by Southwark's bailiffs and officers four times a year. Henry's Ordinance treated the stews just like any other place of public entertainment and the main concern seemed to be that stewholders, or landlords, should not derive an income from the working girls other than rent, and should not entice others into prostitution.

THE RULES

Girls were to be allowed to come and go as they wished; stewholders were not supposed to interact with them and were specifically forbidden to lend the girls money, which could give them a means of control. Stews were technically boarding houses rather than brothels and were not the most convivial of places, as no food, drink or fuel could be sold.

Prostitutes were fined for working when parliament was in session – whether or not to ensure MPs' attendance at Westminster rather than the Bankside brothels is a matter for speculation.

Curious rules included fines for throwing stones or making faces at passers-by. The sums involved were minuscule but such offences were obviously common, as they were regularly recorded in court rolls. The women were also forbidden to wear aprons, to distinguish them from ordinary housewives.

Prostitutes also had to spend all night with their last customer. This seems to have been intended to limit unauthorized river traffic at night, as was the ban on stewholders owning their own boats.

HENRY II

There came a point when Henry needed money for his military campaigns in France. Throughout Europe, countries imposed a *'putage'* or tax on prostitutes, but this would have been unpopular in England, so the canny monarch granted the Bishop of Winchester sixteen properties from the royal estate in Southwark to offer 'ecclesiastical correction'. When the Bishop was unable to enforce law and order he appealed to the king, who was more than happy to step in, but of course, this entitled him to collect the fines which became his unofficial tax.

The fines applied to a number of offences but were generally fairly low, with heavier penalties awarded to the stewholders than to the prostitutes.

THE HAIRCUT OF SHAME

In the fourteenth century, any man convicted of pimping was to have his beard and head shaved, apart from a five centimetre fringe. He was then to be taken to the pillory where he would be kept in the stocks for a period of time agreed by the town elders or mayor. Just to make sure everyone witnessed the event, the journey to the stocks was accompanied by a merry band of minstrels.

Madams or bawds were to be similarly shamed, their hair cut into a short bowl shape. Their trip from prison to the thew, or women's stocks, was a similarly public, riotous affair, to the sound of the minstrels' tune.

COCK'S LANE AND OTHER STREETS

The Golden Boy of Cock Lane marked the spot where the Great
Fire of London ended

Despite attempts to restrict brothels to Bankside, prostitution flourished in many areas of London along with other cities and towns. The street names bear witness; many medieval streets were simply named after the main trade or craft conducted there.

There is little mystery about what went on in the subtly named Gropecunt Lane, a common street name in many towns in the late thirteenth century, Cock's Lane, Codpiece Lane and Maiden Lane. Gropecunt Lane was later sanitized to become Grape

Lane, and in London it was then renamed Grub Street, home to many publishers and newspapers; Cock's Lane often changed to Cook's Lane. In Paris, there were the equally graphic Rue Trousse Puteyne (the 'slut's slit') and Rue du Poil au Con ('street of cunt hair') now called Rue de Pélécan.

LIKE A VIRGIN

Theologians of the day drew up a series of Penitentials to be used as guides for priests hearing confession. These were basically a list of sins and suggestions for the appropriate penance that must be performed in order to gain forgiveness. In the early Middle Ages a number of days spent praying and fasting was the usual penance, although depending upon the gravity of the sin this could involve years of fasting on holy days. For having sex with his wife on a Sunday, for instance, a man was obliged to fast for four days on bread and water. Later on, pardons from sin, or indulgences, could simply be bought from the travelling Pardoner, or other churchmen, making sinning and repentance easier on the stomach.

This strict 'lie back and think of England' message didn't quite fit with medieval doctors' views. Far from female orgasm being a discovery of the sexual revolution of the 1960s, it was generally held that conception was impossible without both male and female orgasm, but most of the methods of achieving it were viewed as sinful.

As long ago as the fourth century BC, classical doctors such as Hippocrates and Galen believed that women as well as men produced semen at the point of orgasm and held that both types were essential if the woman was to become pregnant. Writings left by Avicenna in the eleventh century, and Albert the Great in the thirteenth, show they held the same ideas. In fact, the belief continued to be widely held until Victorian studies of anatomy disproved it.

The ideal was obviously a virgin bride, courted in the proper fashion and married with the father's blessing. The matter was taken very seriously, not least because as well as honour, there was often money in the form of a dowry at stake.

Again, following on from doctors in the classical age, Avicenna and Albert the Great (who was made a saint in 1931) outlined in some detail the exact 'signs of virginity and its corruption', which seems to have provided an extremely useful guide for anyone wanting to 'restore' virginity.

Syringing several times with an astringent solution was said to tighten everything sufficiently to avoid any suspicion. To replicate signs of bleeding it was suggested that a tiny piece of sponge soaked in blood, or a small fish bladder filled with blood, should be inserted into the vagina.

WAYWARD WIVES

Two years after the Norman conquest of Britain in 1066, William the Conqueror and his knights were still fighting to assert control and quell any uprisings. Wives left behind in Normandy were unwilling to make the Channel crossing to a rough-and-ready land with few home comforts but they were nonetheless missing the physical attentions of their husbands. Many sent messages warning in no uncertain terms that unless their husbands returned post haste, they would be forced to take a lover.

William sought to keep his army, promising lands and titles as rewards. Some stayed, but many returned to France, including Humphrey of Tilleul, who gave up Hastings Castle, and his brother-in-law Hugh of Grandmesnil, who renounced the governorship of Winchester. Neither they nor their heirs ever regained the titles or lands they had left behind.

CAMP FOLLOWERS

By 1096 when Pope Urban II called for the First Crusade to recapture Jerusalem, women seem to have overcome their distaste for travel or rough living. Many chose to accompany the crusaders as cooks, laundresses, cleaners and most of all, prostitutes. Many who started out as pilgrims found that selling their favours was the best way to support themselves on the long journey. Maybe they saw it as their duty to support the crusaders in their holy fight against the infidels; certainly many who opted for a change of profession en route were originally nuns.

King Richard I, better known as Richard the Lionheart, urged his troops to stay focused on the battle and was cross with them for wasting so much of his money on women. By the end of the first crusade, the then Pope Clement II issued a decree discouraging women, and particularly attractive young women, from accompanying the armies.

Meanwhile, back at home, abandoned wives presented another moral dilemma for the Church. This quickly became apparent and Pope Urban II wrote a letter shortly after the crusaders set off suggesting that married men should first ask the consent of their wives before they left for the Holy Land.

ENFORCED CHASTITY

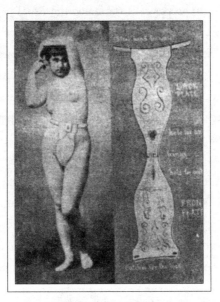

A metal chastity belt

Chastity belts, that mainstay of humour and medieval mockery, seem to have first appeared in the fourteenth century, when they were often called Florentine girdles, although whether they were really developed in Italy is doubtful and probably works along the lines of syphilis being known as the French disease in England and the English disease in France. Jokes about spare keys seem to have developed around the same time. They remained a feature of surgical instrument catalogues until the 1930s.

From the end of the thirteenth century, a staggering proportion of court cases for which records remain were concerned with sex and marriage, mainly fornication, adultery and prostitution. Between 60 and 90 per cent remained the usual pattern for the next three centuries. Punishments varied but often involved public humiliation and beatings, though women were sometimes ordered to give alms to the poor or sent on a pilgrimage. This was supposedly to give the offender time to meditate on her sins but in reality seems to have offered greater opportunity for repeat offending.

BEFORE WE DIE

Far from dampening passion, epidemics of plague, and in particular the Black Death, which ravaged Europe from 1348, wiping out a third of the population, seemed to fan the flames. A spirit of hedonism gripped the population and despite the fact that crowding into taverns and brothels was likely to spread the disease, that's exactly what people did.

Trade thrived, with many believing that intercourse, particularly sex with a prostitute, ensured immunity from infection. There was also a rush to the altar with widows and the unmarried keen to tie the knot before they died.

COURTLY LOVE

Alongside the brothels and bawds, the concept of rarefied courtly love was also evolving. In the early middle ages, women were associated with Eve, the wanton temptress, cause of man's downfall. But returning pilgrims and crusaders brought back Byzantine ideas of devotion to Mary, holy intercessor between man and God, the idealization of femininity and motherhood, who was seen as above sexuality.

This linked with the ideals of courtly or fine love appearing in the poetry and songs of the troubadours of Southern France. The troubadours flourished between 1100 and 1350 attached to various courts. There had been no European tradition of love literature before the twelfth century but visitors to Spain and Sicily were increasingly influenced by the Arabic love poetry and philosophy they heard there.

The theme of ennobling love began to feature in the poems of Guilhem, Count of Poitiers and Duke of Aquitaine, and was taken up by powerful nobles like Eleanor of Aquitaine, Guilhem's granddaughter. She and her daughter Marie of Champagne set up a court in late twelfth-century Poitiers, which was controlled by women. A code of rules was drawn up to teach courtiers how to behave, set down by Marie's chaplain Andreas Capellanus. Courtly love was sensual love for an unobtainable, idealized lady, but it was essentially pure, which prohibited physical consummation – all of the angst, desire and jealousy to incite passion without any physical release. That was the theory. It was probably upheld to a greater degree in northern Europe, where the Church's authority was more likely to result in punishment. In the hotter climate of the south, couples may have got away with rather more.

A TRUE KNIGHT'S TALE

Ulrich von Liechtenstein

Ulrich von Liechtenstein provides an example of chivalry in practice. A thirteenth-century nobleman and knight from the Duchy of Styria in modern-day Austria, he wrote extensively about how knights and nobles might lead more virtuous lives. He is particularly remembered for *Service of Ladies*, an autobiographical collection of poetry in which he tells of the great deeds of honour he performs for married noblewomen, following the strict conventions of chaste courtly love.

He travelled from Venice to Vienna dressed as the goddess Venus. Wearing a selection of elaborate gowns, braids and jewels, he jousted with other knights for the honour of his chosen lady, breaking 307 lances and defeating all opponents. In the true spirit of courtly love his lady remained scornful, demanding further deeds and even mutilation: he apparently offered her his little finger, prettily presented in a velvet box complete with gold clasps. For some reason, this failed to impress. He then embarked on a second quest, this time taking on the more masculine guise of King Arthur, wandering the country attending tournaments.

BARD'S TALES

The Wife of Bath

By the time Gutenberg invented the printing press around 1440, roughly a third of the population could read and write. Until then, books were copied out painstakingly by hand. With limited numbers surviving, fictional works by contemporary authors can offer a valuable insight into what people were really like. One of the best for people-watching is Chaucer's *Canterbury Tales*. He drew on a cast of real characters he'd met travelling extensively in his work as a bureaucrat, diplomat and courtier working first for King Edward III and then for Richard II, and the tales his pilgrims tell are in some cases taken from well-known stories from across Europe; almost every one concludes with a piece of proverbial wisdom.

Chaucer's pilgrims come from all walks of life and appear to be on their pilgrimage for a range of reasons, mostly nothing to do with spirituality or religious fervour. It is fitting they should meet to start their journey at the Tabard Inn in Southwark, a highly dubious area. Amongst the group are several churchmen who embody the general view of them at the time.

The Nun or Prioress, Madame Eglantyne, is described as coy and very refined. She spoke French, but coming from the East End school of Stratford Atte Bowe, she knew nothing of Parisian-style French. Chaucer describes her as 'all sentiment and tender heart' but mainly for her pampered little dogs. There is also some suggestion that she has a secret lover as she wears a gold brooch with a crowned letter 'A', engraved with the motto *Amor vincit omnia* – Love conquers all. The monk is fat and ruddy, a keen hunter, following the modern way of the world and not caring for the idea that hunters cannot be holy men or that a monk should spend much time alone in his cell.

Two of the most memorable characters are the Summoner and the Pardoner. A summoner's job was to bring miscreants before the ecclesiastical courts and they had a general reputation for corruption. Chaucer's Summoner was no exception and he is portrayed as a vile individual with a face livid with carbuncles and pimples, 'hot and lecherous as a sparrow', fond of garlic and onions, small wonder he frightened children. And Chaucer suggests quite crudely that he's attracted to the equally unappealing Pardoner who sold Papal indulgences, many of which were fake. The Pardoner has lank yellow hair, no beard and a high voice, so unmasculine that Chaucer compares him to a gelding or castrated horse.

Then there's the Wife of Bath, five times married 'apart from other company in youth', plus she had travelled to Jerusalem with the crusaders with all the implications for behaviour that carried. Her widowhood gave her a great deal of freedom and her tale is all about women being in control. She's probably looking out for husband number six on the pilgrimage to Canterbury.

And Chaucer himself? He was married to Philippa de Roet, a lady in waiting to Edward III's Queen Philippa of Hainault. They had several children but he never wrote any poetry to her as far as we know. It is just possible that the object of his own unattainable courtly love was Blanche of Lancaster, first wife of Chaucer's patron, John of Gaunt. *The Book of the Duchess* was written in honour of Blanche after her death.

A RENAISSANCE PORNOGRAPHER

Born in Arezzo in 1492, Pietro Aretino achieved considerable wealth and influence through his clever, wittily observed satirical writings and verse. He was forced to flee Rome having scandalized society with his 'Lust Sonnets' describing the sixteen positions depicted in Raimondi's erotic engravings. This was the first time pornographic text and imagery appeared together and the few surviving fragments are in the British Museum.

Aretino's mixture of literary flattery and blackmail enabled him to live in a palazzo on the Grand Canal in Venice which he shared with a number of men as well as women. He died as he lived, enjoying himself immensely. He is said to have laughed so much at a dirty joke told by his sister, that he breathed his last, some claiming he suffocated, others that he fell off his chair, cracking his head.

Aretino was not alone in showing little discrimination between men and women when it came to sexual partners. Although in practice society seemed relaxed, there were strict rules. The Florentines established heterosexual state brothels in 1415 in a bid to encourage young men away from homosexuality and in Venice an edict went out from the Doge that women should dress to impress and expose as much flesh as possible to incite male passions. In France meanwhile, it was called doing it the 'Italian way' and anyone caught in the act and convicted could be executed.

SAINTS AND SINNERS

A true moralist sees no crime in what is natural.
Richard Carlile

While there is some debate as to what exactly the cardinal virtues are, there has been little doubt about the Seven Deadly Sins since Pope Gregory I revised the list at the end of the sixth century: wrath, avarice, gluttony, sloth, pride, lust and envy.

And from the early fourteenth century, writers, artists and people in general were obsessed with the notion of sin. Perhaps inspired by the reality of 'eat, drink and be merry, for tomorrow we die', having witnessed the destruction wrought by the Black Death, the Seven Deadly Sins were frequently depicted in paintings and featured heavily in literature. Dante refers to them in his *Inferno* and St Thomas Aquinas wrote extensively on each.

Just as the Seven Deadly Sins each have their corresponding virtue, so for every sinner there was a saint – in theory, at least – although very often it could be hard to distinguish between the two …

A SAINTLY POPE

Pope Gregory I himself was made a saint shortly after his death in AD 604 and he is usually known as St Gregory the Great. Commonly referred to as the Father of Christian Worship, his body of work revised the practices of Roman Catholic worship. A millennium later, in the sixteenth century, even the anti-papist Protestant reformer John Calvin declared Gregory to have been the last good pope.

It is unlikely that Gregory actually invented the Gregorian chant that is named after him, but nonetheless he is the patron saint of musicians, singers, students and teachers.

HAIR SHIRTS

Medieval saints were very keen on the idea of the mortification of the flesh, the better to commune with the spirit. Hair shirts – or cilices, to give them their proper name – were made from goats' hair or other coarse animal hair and worn next to the skin so as to irritate it. It was thought that this constant discomfort kept the wearer in a state of moral awareness. To make the hair shirt even more uncomfortable, thin wire hooks or twigs were sometimes added.

St Patrick of Ireland reputedly always wore one and Thomas Becket, later St Thomas, was wearing one when he was murdered in Canterbury Cathedral on 29 December 1170. Reports from the time describe how, when he was being prepared for burial, exposure to the cold winter air woke the lice in his hair shirt so that 'it boiled over with them like water in a simmering cauldron'.

Hair shirts were not just popular with saints, however. Chroniclers report many instances of princes and even emperors wearing them, and there were undoubtedly a great many more ordinary wearers whose lives and deaths history does not record.

The Emperor Charlemagne was buried in one in the early ninth century and in 1077 the Holy Roman Emperor Henry IV wore a hair shirt on his penitent 450-mile Walk to Canossa to apologize to Pope Gregory VII for doubting his authority. Prince Henry the Navigator of Portugal, grandson of John of Gaunt, was wearing one when he died in 1460 and the chronicler William of Malmesbury describes how Matilda, mother of the Empress Matilda and grandmother of Henry II of England, generally wore a hair shirt beneath her royal robes. He also adds that, during Lent, she would walk to church barefoot and wash the feet of the diseased.

MEDIEVAL FLAGELLANTS

Flagellants giving themselves a good beating (1493)

Taking bodily discomfort several steps further were the medieval flagellants. For this group of religious fanatics, the discomfort of the hair shirt was not enough. Neither was private repentance and prayer. In an outburst of fervour, several took to the streets, whipping themselves into a state of hysteria before falling prostrate into the dirt. The first reported incidence was in Perugia in Umbria, Italy, in 1259, after a series of crop failures and famine.

This sparked something of a craze, particularly following outbreaks of plague or other natural catastrophes. The flagellants wore white robes and carried heavy crosses as they roamed through the countryside, sometimes adding nails to their whips to better scourge their flesh. Occasionally they would sing to accompany their lashes.

Popular throughout Europe during the thirteenth and

fourteenth centuries, the flagellation movement never really caught on in Britain, although Sir Robert Avesbury described a march of about 600 flagellants descending on London in 1349 when the Black Death was raging.

The flagellants were eventually denounced as heretics by the Catholic Church in the late fourteenth century, and when it looked as if there might be a revival of the movement in the fifteenth century the Inquisition was quick to suppress it.

ALL FOR LOVE

To a modern reader, the 900-year-old tale of Héloïse and Abélard seems to contain elements of both saint and sinner. It is a true story of passion, betrayal and lovers torn apart, and the lovers paid a cruel price for their liaison.

Héloïse was a brilliant and beautiful scholar in early-twelfth-century Paris, the cherished niece of Canon Fulbert of Notre-Dame Cathedral. Proud of his young charge and keen to encourage her sharp intellect, Fulbert appointed one of the brightest and most popular philosophers and theologians of the day, Pierre Abélard, as her tutor.

Tutor and pupil got along all too well. Before long, Abélard, claiming the care of his household and financial concerns were interfering with his studies, moved into Fulbert and Héloïse's house. Inevitably the two became lovers; as Abélard wrote: 'We were first together in one house and then one in mind.' The couple took full advantage of their time alone together when they were supposed to be hard at study.

Although Abélard was probably some twenty years older than his young lover, there is no doubt he and Héloïse were equally matched in passion and wit. Letters between them discovered in 1980 show two people trying to outdo each other's declarations of love with their own assertions of adoration.

By the time Fulbert discovered their illicit affair, Héloïse was already pregnant. The lovers escaped to Abélard's sister's house in Brittany, where their son, Astrolabe, was born. Abélard returned to Fulbert and begged forgiveness, asking his permission to marry Héloïse.

Still furious, Fulbert agreed, but Héloïse was reluctant, fearing Abélard's reputation and career would be ruined. As a clergyman, Abélard was strictly forbidden to marry.

After much persuasion, she agreed they should marry in secret. Astrolabe was left with his aunt, Abélard's sister, and Héloïse went to stay with the nuns at the Convent of Argenteuil, whence Héloïse prophetically wrote to him: 'Then there is no more left than this, that in our doom the sorrow yet to come shall be no less than the love we two have already known.'

Perhaps believing that Abélard had abandoned Héloïse, Fulbert began leaking rumours of their marriage, which Héloïse vehemently denied. Their story then takes a rather shocking turn: after bribing Abélard's servant, Fulbert and other relatives sent thugs to brutally attack and castrate Abélard. A lesser man might have died of his wounds but just weeks later, at Abélard's insistence, the lovers took vows of celibacy and retired from the world, Abélard to the monastery of St Denis and Heloise back to the Convent of Argenteuil.

Héloïse became a prioress and for years had no contact with Abélard, but in the 1120s she became an abbess at the Oratory of the Paraclete, which Abélard had established just outside Paris. Although his work took him elsewhere, they struck up a regular correspondence inspired by Abélard's account of their relationship. Héloïse wrote to him frequently, revealing the continuing strength and passion of her love.

'They do not know the hypocrite I am,' she wrote. 'I should be groaning over the sins I have committed but I can only sigh for what I have lost ... Lewd visions take such a hold upon my unhappy soul my thoughts are on their wantonness instead of my prayers ...

'I never sought anything in you except yourself ... I looked for no marriage bond.'

In her letters Héloïse was self-sacrificing, idealistic and noble, but at the same time intriguingly unconventional and boldly naughty. She never stopped loving Abélard, and this is perhaps the real key as to why their story still resonates.

'For me,' she went on, 'youth and passion and experience of pleasures which were so delightful intensify the torments of the flesh and longings of desire, and the assault is the more overwhelming as the nature they attack is the weaker ...

'If Augustus, emperor of the whole world, saw fit to honour me with marriage and conferred all the earth on me to possess forever, it would be dearer and more honourable to me to be called not his empress but your whore.'

Alas, Abélard's writings indicated he no longer felt the same way – perhaps unsurprisingly, given his mutilation. He claimed that what he felt was driven by lust, not love, and that it was a sin. They should both be directing their passions towards their religion, he felt. In her desire to maintain a relationship, even if it could not be the one she would like, Héloïse set aside her own feelings and instead wrote to Abélard on the only topics that would interest him. She was always an excellent student and for the next twenty years she questioned him on matters of biblical and moral principle and philosophy.

Héloïse inspired Abélard's best work, ensuring he would be remembered as one of his century's greatest thinkers. In return, his thoughts, confidences and confessions were all written to Héloïse. His final wish was to be buried where she would be near him.

There is some debate about whether or not Abélard got his wish. They were supposedly both buried at the Oratory of the Paraclete but in 1817 transferred by Empress Josephine, who was moved by their tragic tale, to a crypt in Paris's Père Lachaise Cemetery. Of course both cemeteries claim to this day to be the 'official' resting place of the original star-crossed lovers. As for poor little Astrolabe, there is just one reference to him in the surviving correspondence: a letter in which Peter the Venerable, who defended Abélard and was to grant him absolution after his death, at Héloïse's request, wrote to Héloïse offering to find her son a post in one of the great churches.

A SIMPLE COUNTRY PARSON

Today Montaillou is a small rural French village in the foothills of the Pyrenees. In many respects it was much the same in the fourteenth century: a fairly typical village of some 250 occupants. But as one of the bastions of Catharism – or the Albigensian heresy, which opposed the corruption of the Catholic Church – it came under the exceedingly close scrutiny of the Inquisition.

Jacques Fournier, the local bishop who went on to become Pope Benedict XII, conducted the investigations, interviewing the villagers about every intimate detail of their lives. He kept copious notes and, when he moved to Rome, took them with him and they remained there in the Vatican Library. They offer an extraordinary insight into everyday life, not just of Montaillou but of all the other similar villages of the period.

The figure of local priest Pierre Clergue stands out from the accounts of village life, and he became the central character in Emmanuel Le Roy Ladurie's history of the village, which was compiled from Fournier's records. Clergue came from a family of wealthy local peasants and was himself a Cathar, although he seems to have avoided punishment for years by informing on other parishioners, effectively controlling who was imprisoned. He also took full advantage of his position to acquire dozens of lovers. An educated man, he knew how to be charming and flatter women; Fournier's notes suggest there was hardly a woman in the area who had not succumbed to his attentions at some point.

At the time, celibacy for priests was not strictly enforced in this region of France – although all sex was sinful, according to Cathar beliefs, particularly in marriage. The promise of deathbed absolution apparently cleared Clergue's conscience on all counts and he pursued new conquests with vigour.

One of his most notable lovers was Béatrice de Planissoles, a wealthy widow and chatelaine of Montaillou. She had previously spurned Clergue's cousin's advances but seemed happy to meet the priest in the church, where he would thoughtfully make up a bed for them to share. She described how he always made her wear a necklace of herbs to prevent pregnancy but never told her exactly what was included in the mixture – presumably, she suspected, to prevent her from using it as protection with other lovers.

Clergue's cousin Grazide Fauré was another of his conquests. She became his mistress at the age of fifteen or sixteen and a year later married Pierre Lizier at Clergue's suggestion. The affair between Grazide and Clergue continued for some years and, when asked if she thought it was a sin, she replied that she did not think it could be, 'nor do I think it could displease God because Pierre and I both enjoyed it'.

Another mistress was Raymonde Vital, who had worked as a servant in the home of one of the wealthier families in Montaillou and was unhappily married to a cobbler, who ignored her for a string of mistresses. Fortunately for her, her husband eventually died and she was free to marry again.

Pierre Clergue's luck finally ran out and he was arrested in 1320.

He eventually died in prison, although there is no record of him ever testifying before the Inquisition.

THE ORIGINAL COUGAR

Béatrice de Planissoles' affair with Pierre Clergue of Montaillou lasted around two years, after which she left the village to marry a minor nobleman called Otho Lagleize of Dalou, with whom she had several children. Following his death, Béatrice had an affair with Barthélemy Amilhac, another priest many years her junior. They ran away together and went through some form of marriage ceremony, although the relationship ended because Barthélemy was concerned that their liaison might draw suspicion due to her previous links with the Cathars. Béatrice's father had been convicted of supporting the Cathar heresy. In the event, Barthélemy was right to worry, for they were both arrested.

Béatrice appeared before Jacques Fournier and the Inquisition to answer charges of blasphemy, witchcraft and heresy. Many of the charges of blasphemy and heresy related to overheard conversations that were supposed to have taken place years earlier, some dating back to the time of her first marriage and none of them conclusive. But the contents of her purse could be viewed as suggestive of spells or sorcery: there were two dried umbilical cords from her grandchildren and blood-soaked linens, said to be her daughters' first menstrual blood, to be made into potions for their husbands to drink to ensure their enduring love. There was also frankincense as a cure for headaches and various herbs including rocket, which was said to increase sexual vigour, together with other folk remedies. Fournier would have recognized most of these as innocent charms and love potions. Surprisingly, the most damning evidence proved to be an innocuous-looking piece of dried bread, which was suspected of being a religious token indicating Cathar sympathies.

Both Barthélemy and Béatrice were imprisoned for over a year, from March 1321 to July 1322. After her release, Béatrice was forced to wear a yellow cross for ever as a punishment, to signal her heretical Cathar beliefs. This was the usual sentence for a Cathar's first offence and was strictly enforced. Anyone persisting in their heresy would be dealt with more severely, usually culminating in execution.

THE INQUISITION

The medieval Inquisition was initially set up by the Catholic Church in twelfth-century France to fight heresy. It was specifically a reaction to Catharism, which was widespread in the south and was regarded as heretical. The first Inquisition was established in 1184, in the Languedoc region of France, as a temporary council. This was later made permanent and placed under the control of the Dominicans in Rome and Carcassonne. After 1200 a Grand Inquisitor headed each Inquisition and anyone accused would first appear before a tribunal; depending upon the outcome, he or she might then face trial.

Aside from religious beliefs, investigations often focused on immoral behaviour and sexual sins as signifiers of heresy. Punishments included execution (usually being burnt at the stake), imprisonment and banishment, with prisoners often tortured first; Pope Innocent IV's papal bull of 1252 explicitly authorized the use of torture against heretics. The system was obviously open to abuse, and as the mere hint or rumour against someone was sufficient to see them summoned before a tribunal, anyone with a grudge could see off their enemy with a whisper to the right person.

THE SPANISH INQUISITION

Two Dominican monks burned at the stake by the Inquisition for
allegedly signing pacts with the Devil (1549)

The most notorious manifestation of the Catholic Inquisition that
aimed to maintain orthodoxy across Europe in the later Middle
Ages was the Spanish Inquisition. Set up in 1481 by Ferdinand
II of Aragon and Isabella I of Castile, the Tribunal of the Holy
Office of the Inquisition in Spain was surprisingly resilient and
survived in some form until 1834, when it was finally abolished
by Isabella II.

Unlike its predecessor, the Spanish Inquisition was controlled
by the Spanish monarchs rather than by the Pope, and they came
down particularly harshly on people of other faiths – it was
around this time that Spain finally wrested control of Andalusia
from the Islamic Moors, a territory in which there was also a
significant Jewish population.

Jews and Muslims were ordered to convert or leave, and many were forced into exile. Those accused of being Protestant were more often burned if found guilty. After the first six people were burned alive in Seville on 6 February 1481, auto-da-fé became a particular feature of the new regime and the Inquisition was extremely active from then until 1530. The trials continued through the rest of the sixteenth century, although the Inquisition was generally less repressive. Around 200 people were accused of being Protestants in the last few decades of the sixteenth century, a considerable reduction on the many hundreds who had previously been convicted and executed.

The witch-hunt in Spain was far less intense than in other parts of Europe – notably Germany, France and Scotland where witchcraft was viewed as a major heresy – but other offences came under the scrutiny of the Inquisition. Any deviation from the straight and narrow was a sin, and sins had to be punished. Better to burn the body but save the soul.

Blasphemy was a very common misdemeanour and covered religious beliefs, sexual morality and immoral behaviour including that of the clergy, although there were rarely severe punishments. Bigamy seems to have been widely practised, presumably because it was almost impossible to obtain a divorce. For men the penalty was five years serving in a royal galley, which amounted to a death sentence; women were also not infrequently implicated and were usually imprisoned if found guilty.

Despite a papal ruling that sodomy was only relevant to the Inquisition if linked to religious heresy, the Spanish Inquisition made it a priority. As was the case elsewhere at the time, sodomy included heterosexual as well as homosexual anal sex, rape, and bestiality. The Tribunal of Zaragoza was notably severe, interrogating 101 men in an eight-year period in the 1570s, and executing at least thirty-five. The final execution for sodomy took place there in April 1633, and records suggest that overall the Inquisition tribunal had convicted around 1,000 for the offence and burnt 170 – 84 of those for bestiality.

THE BORGIAS

Greed, corruption, lust, murder, intrigue: the story of the Borgias has it all, and since their heyday in the fifteenth and sixteenth centuries the family name has become synonymous with cruelty and debauchery.

The Borgias, or Borjas, as they were originally known, came from Valencia, at that time in the kingdom of Aragon. The first to come to prominence was Alfonso, who was a professor of law and a diplomat before becoming Pope Calixtus III in 1455 at the age of seventy-seven. He seems to have been quite honest, certainly by the standards of the time, although he did advance the interests of his own family, including his nephew Rodrigo, who was made a cardinal at the young age of twenty-five.

RODRIGO BORGIA

When Calixtus died in 1458, Rodrigo soon found himself a new ally in the next pope, Pius II, and he set about acquiring Church benefices and land, adding to his wealth and power. He was also building a reputation for promiscuity and was rebuked several times by Pius. This evidently had no effect, for, by the time Rodrigo became Pope Alexander VI in 1492, he had fathered eight children by at least three different women.

The four with whom he was closest, and who share his infamy, were Giovanni, Cesare, Lucrezia and Gioffre, all by his long-term illicit mistress, the aristocrat Vanozza dei Catanei.

Once pope, Alexander openly set about promoting his children and family, bestowing appointments, land and riches upon them. He made his favoured elder son Giovanni commander-in-chief of the papal army, Cesare a cardinal, and, in a bid to create dynastic alliances, twelve-year-old Lucrezia was married to Giovanni Sforza of the powerful Milanese ruling family while Gioffre was married to Sancha of Aragon. He moved their mother, Vanozza, to the papal court and later settled his young mistress, Giulia Farnese, into a palace next to the Vatican to live with Lucrezia.

Alexander intended that Giovanni should take the throne of Naples but his ambitions came to an end when Giovanni was found dead in the River Tiber. His throat had been cut and there were nine stab wounds to his body. He was only twenty, but his violent and unstable character, and his constant dalliances with other men's wives – including, it is said, his brother Gioffre's –

had earned him many enemies. From the first, suspicion for the murder has always fallen upon his brother Cesare. They were possibly rivals for their sister-in-law Sancha, or even for their sister Lucrezia, and it is a strange fact that Alexander, although genuinely devastated by his son's death, was content for nobody ever to be convicted or even formally accused of his murder. Given his character, it is also remarkable that Cesare would not have wrought vengeance on the perpetrator.

CESARE BORGIA

Cesare certainly benefited from his brother's death, taking over his position as favoured son and heir and amassing greater wealth and power. He persuaded Alexander to release him from his religious vows, becoming the first man ever to relinquish his cardinal's hat. He was appointed papal envoy to France, where he was made Duke of Valentinois and married Princess Charlotte, a relative of King Louis XIII, with whom he had a son. Returning to Italy, Cesare set about asserting Borgia family control in the papal states.

The Venetian ambassador reported back of him, 'Every night four or five men are discovered assassinated, bishops, prelates and others, so that all Rome trembles for fear of being murdered by the Duke.'

LUCREZIA BORGIA

Lucrezia Borgia

Giovanni Sforza was proving a less than useful ally or soldier, and so his marriage to Lucrezia was annulled in December 1497 on the grounds that it had never been consummated. Lucrezia, however, was six months pregnant and a son, Giovanni, was born in secret in March 1498. The mysterious child's existence was not made public for three years, allowing all sorts of speculation to surface. Also known as the Infans Romanus, or Child of Rome, young Giovanni Borgia was the subject of two papal decrees, the first stating he was the illegitimate son of Cesare and the second that he was the illegitimate son of Alexander – neither admitting that Lucrezia was the mother and both fuelling rumours of incest.

Cesare may or may not have ordered the murder of Lucrezia's supposed lover Perotto, whose body was flung into the Tiber in

February 1498 along with that of the maid who had purportedly helped the lovers meet. Not only did Perotto stand in the way of a dynastic marriage, but there were also whispers that he was little Giovanni's father and that Cesare was jealous of his influence.

In another political alliance, Lucrezia was then married to Prince Alfonso of Aragon. This soon clashed with Cesare's ambitions to strengthen relations with France and break with the kingdom of Naples, so the young Prince Alfonso was duly despatched. He survived being stabbed in July 1500 but while recovering from his injuries he was strangled. Cesare was almost certainly behind both attempts.

Lucrezia has often been portrayed as a skilled poisoner and rumours of incest with Cesare have persisted to modern times. Recently historians have cast her in a more favourable light as another victim of her family's intrigues and deception, a useful pawn in their political schemes.

DEBAUCHERY

And then there were the reports of debauchery and excess. The so-called Banquet of Chestnuts in October 1501 was particularly decisive in sealing the Borgias' reputation.

Bishop Johann Burchard, master of ceremonies for the pope – who, lest we forget, was himself a Borgia – recorded in his diary how fifty prostitutes and courtesans attended the meal, after which they danced, at first fully dressed and then naked. Candles were distributed about the room and then the floor was scattered with chestnuts, which the naked dancers crawled about to collect. Pope Alexander, Cesare and Lucrezia Borgia watched as prizes of silken doublets, shoes and hats were then offered to those men who could 'perform' most frequently with the prostitutes in this very public orgy.

Burchard also records how the three Borgias watched from a balcony as rampant stallions raged at each other in a fenced courtyard in St Peter's Square, before tearing across to some captive mares, wounding themselves and the mares in the process.

Disfigured by syphilis towards the end of his relatively short life, Cesare wore a mask whenever he appeared in public. Nevertheless, even at the height of his notoriety, he was admired for his boundless energy and courage and could be charming when he chose. He fathered at least eleven illegitimate children with a variety of partners.

THE END OF THE STORY

In August 1503, both Alexander and Cesare were struck down with fever. Cesare recovered but the seventy-two-year-old pope did not. There were suspicions of poisoning but they had most likely contracted malaria. Rome in summer was hot and unhealthy, and the disease was rife.

Cesare's position was no longer secure and, although he tried to effect a deal with Pope Julius II, they became bitter enemies.

He was killed in battle in 1507 besieging a castle in Navarre. He was just thirty-two.

Lucrezia lived on with her third husband, Alfonso d'Este, Duke of Ferrara, with whom she had several children. As Duchess of Ferrara from 1505, Lucrezia established a reputation as a patron of the arts, presiding over a flourishing artistic community in the state. She died aged thirty-nine in 1519 of complications following the stillbirth of a daughter.

Infamous in their lifetimes, the Borgias were almost certainly guilty of a string of the most outrageous crimes, including bribery, corruption, theft, murder, poisonings, rape, and possibly incest to complete the list. Whilst in no way compensating for their wrongdoings, it could on a more saintly note be argued that Alexander's shrewd diplomacy and administration, not to mention his financial provisions, ensured the survival of the papacy at a time when it was far from secure. Along with other powerful and similarly ruthless families of their day, the Borgias were also generous benefactors and patrons who contributed to the culture of their era; without them some of the greatest art of the Renaissance would never have been produced.

The Borgias' influence continued through the sixteenth century, although rather more quietly. Several held religious and political positions, and Francis Borgia, who lived from 1510 to 1572, was even made a saint.

MARRIAGE AND THE REFORMATION

Martin Luther was an important reformer and seminal figure in the Protestant Reformation of the sixteenth century, which changed the course of the Christian religion, not to mention European and world history.

Luther was born on 10 November 1483 in Eisleben, Saxony. After a university education he enrolled in law school but found himself increasingly drawn to theology and philosophy. He entered a closed Augustinian friary in Erfurt in 1505 and was ordained a priest in 1507. Five years later he joined the theological faculty at the University of Wittenberg. It was there, in 1517, that he composed his revolutionary *Ninety-Five Theses on the Power and Efficacy of Indulgences*, attacking papal abuses and the sale of indulgences. Thanks to the development of the printing press, Luther's writings spread quickly throughout Europe and were to provide the initial catalyst for the Protestant Reformation. He went on to translate the Bible into German, which had a profound impact on German culture and language, and helped to inspire the composition of the King James Bible over in England. He also wrote hymns for inclusion in church services, something of a revolution back in the day.

Luther had long condemned vows of celibacy for priests, although he believed he himself would never marry: 'My mind is averse to wedlock because I daily expect the death of a heretic.' That said, in 1525, two years after helping a group of disillusioned nuns escape from a Catholic convent hidden among the herring barrels on a fish wagon, Luther married Katharina von Bora, one of the escapees.

Their marriage seems to have been a successful and happy one. Luther said a little over a year after their wedding, 'My Katie is in all things so obliging and pleasing to me that I would not exchange my poverty for the riches of Croesus.'

The couple had six children, four of whom survived, and they also brought up four orphans. Katharina helped boost the family income by farming and taking in boarders at their home, the Black Cloister, a former monastery given them as a wedding present. She also ran a hospital with other nurses on the site.

SEX WITHIN MARRIAGE

Alongside the changes to doctrine and worship, Martin Luther and Protestantism affected attitudes towards sex and marriage. A far greater importance was placed upon sex within marriage, which was no longer regarded as a sin. Marriage itself was treated as a loving union, even a sacred duty, rather than something akin to a business alliance. When Luther heard that his good friend George Spalatin, another former priest, was about to get married, he was delighted and wrote to congratulate him, adding, 'When you sleep with your Catherine and embrace her, you should think, "This child of man, this wonderful creature of God, has been given to me by my Christ. May he be praised and glorified." On the evening of the day on which, according to my calculations, you will receive this, I shall make love to my Katharina while you make love to yours and thus we will be united in love.'

The frank and open references to sexual love seem to have been typical at this time.

THE WAGES OF SIN

The outbreaks of plague that had decimated the European population throughout the Middle Ages had conversely also served as a call to pleasure without consequence, encouraging sexual licence and promiscuity in the face of death.

The new pestilence that swept through the Renaissance world in the late fifteenth century was viewed differently, however. Seen as a judgement on sinners, it seemed the only answer was to repent and reform.

THE POX

The earliest known portrayal of pox victims (1498)

The 'great pox' that ravaged Europe for a number of decades from 1495 onwards was an epidemic of syphilis. The symptoms were noted among French troops besieging Naples, and when they returned to France they took the infection with them. The disease was officially recorded in Naples in January 1496. Just two months later there were sufficient cases in Paris for the authorities to attempt to control it, although it nonetheless seems to have arrived in England around the turn of the sixteenth century.

At first the pox was blamed on Columbus's sailors returning from the New World with a virulent new disease against which the Europeans had no immunity. Many Spanish mercenaries who had sailed with Columbus were among the French troops who marched into Italy in 1495, although the pox's rapid spread would imply that the fifty or so crewmembers had been extremely busy when they first got back from America.

Other theories circulated as to its origins, which are still hotly debated by medical historians. Some claimed an existing mild disease had mutated to become pathogenic, others that the pox had existed before but had simply been misdiagnosed as leprosy. One of the wilder ideas of the day came from Francis Bacon, who thought it was the result of cannibalism in the West Indies.

Meanwhile, everyone blamed everyone else: the French called it the Neapolitan sickness, the Italians, the Spanish and the British all called it the French disease, the Russians called it the Polish disease, and the Germans referred to it as Spanish scabies.

Pope Alexander VI's physician, Dr Pedro Pinto, described the pox as 'an obscene disease: dire flames upon their vitals fed within, while Sores and crusted Filth prophan'd their Skin'. He would have treated the pope's son Cesare Borgia, who caught the pox when he was in France.

The Italian poet and physician Girolamo Fracastoro was responsible for the disease's official name, syphilis. In his poem *Syphilis sive morbus gallicus* (*Syphilis, or the French disease*), Syphilis, a Greek peasant, becomes ill and develops ulcers over his body after angering Apollo. He is cured by Mercury, god of medicine.

Whether it was a completely new disease or a mutated version of an existing one, the strain of syphilis that struck Europe in the late fifteenth century was extraordinarily severe and deadly in its rapid spread. In a book on the subject published in 1539, Ruy

Diaz de Isla estimated that over one million people were infected across Europe.

Seventeenth-century English physician Thomas Sydenham described some of the more hideous symptoms in great detail in a letter to Henry Paman. First a small red spot appeared on the genitals, followed by a discharge from the urethra. A painful ulcer developed, followed by swellings or buboes in the lymph nodes of the groin. Headaches and universal pain were next, and then sores all over the body. The bones of the skull, legs and arms developed raised nodules and mucus membranes, soft tissue and cartilage were eaten away by tumours, particularly the nose. Many other contemporary accounts describe those infected as being covered from head to knees with stinking, suppurating sores, the flesh literally falling from their faces.

By the time Thomas Sydenham was writing, the disease had lost some of its virulence, possibly through better hygiene and living standards, or because the population had developed a degree of immunity. This brought its own problems, however, as it was easier to hide any signs of infection. People were not always aware they had been infected, and once the initial sore disappeared and syphilis entered a period of dormancy many thought they were cured. The disease was then passed on to other sexual partners and children who were born with congenital syphilis, causing all sorts of health troubles and deformities.

CLOSURE OF THE BROTHELS

The sex trade was generally blamed for the spread of diseases including gonorrhoea and other infections, but the horror and scale of this new epidemic sweeping the continent led to appeals for the closure of brothels, and calls for a new moral order. None of the regulations that were passed succeeded in reducing prostitution, however. Closure simply widened the problem as women now plied their trade in the streets. In 1490, the official register recorded 7,000 prostitutes in Rome and over 11,000 in Venice; these numbers did not alter following legislation.

In England, Henry VII attempted to close brothels in all the major cities in 1504. According to *The Survey of London*, written by the Elizabethan historian John Stow, the whitewashed 'stews' on London's Bankside, with names such as The Crane, The Bell, The Cardinal's Cap and The Swan, shut briefly but soon reopened – albeit with slightly fewer in-house prostitutes as many had scattered throughout the city and suburbs.

HENRY VIII: GUARDIAN OF MORALITY

It was Henry VII's son, Henry VIII, who passed the two strictest laws limiting sexual freedom. The first was the Buggery Act of 1533, steered through parliament by Henry's chief minister Thomas Cromwell.

Buggery was defined as an unnatural sexual act and included

sodomy, incest, bestiality and even witchcraft. The act basically covered any unconventional sex act and Henry VIII and the Tudors found it an extremely useful cover-all against their many enemies. Buggery was denounced as a crime against the king, punishable by death and the ignominy of burial without religious rites. The act remained on the statute books until the nineteenth century.

Then, in April 1546, Henry VIII ordered the closure of London's stews and all the 'houses of prostitution' within his kingdom. An edict was sent out, literally trumpeted by heralds on the streets, that the brothels were to close at once. Popular related medieval entertainments, including dogfighting and bearbaiting, were to cease immediately, too.

The law stated its intention to end the 'toleration of such dissolute and miserable persons as have been suffered to dwell in common open places called the stews without punishment or correction for their abominable and detestable sin'. It was all somewhat hypocritical, of course, given Henry's own fondness for the company of what were euphemistically known as 'Winchester geese' – not that he frequented the stews. It is thought women were usually procured for him by Archbishop Stephen Gardiner, former Bishop of Winchester, who was himself afflicted with the disease in 1553. There is still disagreement over whether or not Henry's own health problems in later life, his bouts of impotence and failure to produce a strong male heir were a result of syphilis.

Just as elsewhere in Europe, the laws made little impact; in fact, they arguably made matters worse. Supervision of public morality was more difficult as many prostitutes moved into alehouses or taverns, and their trade became more illicit and widespread. At least two of the stews mentioned by John Stow remained in business in Shakespeare's time, later in the sixteenth century. Whitewashed and with their signs still in evidence, The Cardinal's Cap and The Bell were conveniently close to several theatres and were a popular haunt of actors and audiences alike.

BRIDEWELL

Bridewell prison in 1667

Public opinion was changing, however, and there was a general hardening of attitudes. In some places, notorious prostitutes were banished and faced flogging and branding if they dared return, and sexual miscreants might be forced to wear special yellow and green collars as a sign of their disgrace.

Many city authorities routinely whipped prostitutes and shaved their heads before carting them through the streets while a jeering crowd threw rotten vegetables and clattered barbers' shaving bowls. Another form of ritual humiliation involved offenders being paraded to the public whipping posts and left for the night in the stocks. In 1550, Lord Mayor of London Rowland Hill widened the use of carting for anyone found guilty of unchastity, including wealthy citizens. It was not a popular move.

Worst of all was Bridewell in London, the first English 'house of correction' designed to deal with prostitutes, the sexually immoral, vagrants and petty criminals. Built in the style of Hampton Court on the banks of the River Thames close to Blackfriars Bridge, Bridewell had originally been one of Henry VIII's palaces. In 1552, his son Edward VI donated it to the city as a place to reform offenders.

There were no real sentences and, once inside, inmates remained there unless someone bailed them out. A combination of prison and workhouse, Bridewell was full of manacles, stocks, blocks to beat out hemp, and treadmills. Those too weak for hard labour made mattresses. Others, more fortunate, were taught to grind corn or shoe horses.

Punishments, however, were sadistic – particularly for women. They were regularly whipped in front of the governors, and beatings, starvation and even gang rape were not uncommon.

As the model for a house of correction, 'Bridewell' became the usual name for similar institutions in cities up and down the country.

RAMPANT ROYALS

*Nothing has been more fatal to men, and to great men,
than the letting themselves go to the forbidden love of
women.* King James II

From time immemorial men, and women, have indulged in illicit
liaisons, and royals everywhere are no exception. In fact they've
probably had more than their fair share of dalliances. There's
nothing quite like power, position and wealth for adding a dash
of extra sex appeal, and when that power is combined with a
royal title the result is evidently a potent aphrodisiac. Over the
centuries there has never been a shortage of willing candidates
for the position of royal mistress or lover.

HENRY VIII

Ask anyone to name a rampant royal and most people will
mention King Henry VIII. You've only got to look at portraits of
the mature king to know he was a man of prodigious appetites
of all descriptions. Like his distant twenty-first-century descendant
Prince Charles, Henry was fairly unusual in his desire to actually
marry his mistress. One can only wonder, had mobile phones
existed in the sixteenth century, what recordings of Henry VIII's
intimate conversations might have revealed. Instead the king –
married at the time to his first wife, Catherine of Aragon, the

widow of his deceased elder brother – wrote his lover Anne Boleyn numerous devotional letters signed with the initials HR (for Henry Rex) on either side of a heart inscribed AB.

Henry VIII's signature on a love letter to Anne Boleyn,
'HR seeks no other'

So smitten was Henry with the strikingly vivacious Anne Boleyn that he was willing to break with Rome, risk eternal damnation through excommunication, and push through a radical overhaul of the established Church. England would never be the same again, and all in order that Henry could get his divorce and make the love of his life his bride. (Well, until she too failed to produce a male heir, and wife number three appeared on the scene.)

Anne had spent several years as a lady-in-waiting at the French court and she attracted many admirers when she returned to England in 1522, both for her looks and for her sophisticated wit and intelligence. Henry had already had an affair with her sister Mary, which resulted in the birth of a child, and when he first turned his attentions to Anne she resisted. This merely served to make him more determined and he showered the Boleyn family with gifts and titles. Anne was made Marchioness of Pembroke in 1532 and by early 1533 she was pregnant with Henry's child. Forced to act fast, he married her in a secret ceremony in January and immediately split from the Catholic Church, passing the Act of Supremacy to declare himself head of the English Church.

A lavish ceremony at Westminster Abbey in June 1533 crowned Anne Queen of England and their daughter Elizabeth was born in September 1533. Less than three years later, on 19 May 1536, Anne was executed at the Tower of London, a victim of the Buggery Act passed in the year of her marriage.

A QUEEN'S DOWNFALL

Following Elizabeth's birth, two further pregnancies, in the summer of 1534 and in January 1536, ended in miscarriage. The public had never taken to Anne, preferring her predecessor Catherine of Aragon, and soon rumours were circulating that she was a witch with six fingers. The stillbirths were taken as further evidence of her guilt.

Henry seems not to have been immune from such wild speculation. When he discovered the second miscarried baby had been a boy he became convinced the marriage was cursed, and he even blamed his bouts of impotence on Anne, since witches were said to cause the condition.

By this time, Anne had also disagreed with Thomas Cromwell, Henry's right-hand man, over political matters and so her fate was sealed. Cromwell and Henry tore her character apart and accused her of the crime of buggery, which at the time was taken to mean any sexual act that might displease God. Next they needed proof of her unnatural sex crimes.

Anne's young Flemish musician, Mark Smeeton, was arrested in April 1536 and tortured until he confessed to having had sex with her. Sir Henry Norris, Sir Francis Weston and William Brereton made similar confessions under torture, and even Anne's brother, Lord George Rochford, was charged with incest, the stillborn son held to be evidence of their union.

Her own father and her uncle, the Duke of Norfolk, were part of the secret commission that investigated her 'crimes'.

At her trial, Anne was accused of adultery and witchcraft, convicted and imprisoned in the Tower of London. She was the first English queen to be publicly executed, though as a special 'mercy' she was beheaded by a French swordsman rather than the usual axe. Perhaps unbelievably, her final speech praised her husband: 'A more merciful prince was there never; and to me he was ever a good, a gentle, and sovereign lord.'

Any grief Henry might have felt for the former love of his life was short-lived. The next day he became betrothed to her successor, Jane Seymour, whom he married on 30 May at the Palace of Whitehall.

THE FLANDERS MARE

With just one surviving (legitimate) male heir, young Prince Edward, Henry was keen to make certain of the continuance of his line; and so, on the death of Jane Seymour, he sought another wife. Impressed by Hans Holbein's flattering portrait, Henry chose the German princess Anne of Cleves.

On meeting his bride on Blackheath, Henry was taken aback by her appearance. 'She is nothing as fair as she hath been reported,' he complained. Nevertheless, encouraged by Thomas Cromwell, who had arranged matters, he determined to go ahead with marriage to 'the Flanders mare', as he dubbed her. Not to have done so would have damaged his alliance with Germany.

The couple were married at the Palace of the Placentia in Greenwich on 6 January 1540. The wedding night was not a success. The next morning Henry told Cromwell, 'I liked her before not well, but now I like her much worse.' He disliked her smell, found her physically repellent and did not believe she was a virgin. There are no reports of what Anne thought of her charming new husband.

The marriage was annulled on the grounds of non-consummation in July that same year and Anne received a generous settlement, including several estates. Afterwards she was referred to as 'the King's Beloved Sister', was a frequent visitor at court and outlived all of Henry's other wives. Thomas Cromwell fared less well: he was executed for treason and heresy on 28 July 1540 as a direct consequence of the disastrous marriage.

DIVORCED, BEHEADED, DIED, DIVORCED, BEHEADED, SURVIVED

Henry's fifth wife, Catherine Howard, was to suffer the same fate as her cousin Anne Boleyn – the difference being that, in Catherine's case, the queen was almost certainly guilty of adultery.

The beautiful young Catherine had been brought up in the free and easy household of her aunt, the Dowager Duchess of Norfolk, where casually licentious behaviour was the norm. There she had fallen into two relationships, with the musician Henry Manox and the household secretary Francis Dereham, whom she possibly intended to marry. The match did not meet with the duchess's approval.

Dispatched to Henry's court, Catherine soon caught the eye of the ageing king. He made her his wife immediately after the annulment of his marriage to Anne of Cleves and the lively Catherine seems to have revived the king's spirits and ardour. He recovered from the impotence that had afflicted him since his previous wedding night and referred to Catherine as his 'rose without a thorn'.

By contrast, Henry now weighed around 140 kilograms (twenty-one stone) and had a festering ulcer on his leg. He was also three decades older than his bride. Perhaps unsurprisingly, the young queen still enjoyed the company of younger men. She flirted with Henry's favoured courtier, Thomas Culpeper, and met him for secret assignations. She also made the mistake of appointing her former lover, Francis Dereham, her secretary.

Reports of Catherine's indiscretions were brought to Archbishop Cranmer, who informed the king. At first Henry refused to believe the accusations but he agreed to authorize an investigation, in which enough evidence was gathered to damn the queen. Culpeper and Dereham confessed, probably under torture, and both were executed – Culpeper was beheaded and Dereham was hanged, drawn and quartered – and subsequently had their heads staked out on London Bridge. Catherine was beheaded at Tower Green on 13 February 1542 and buried near her infamous cousin in the chapel of St Peter ad Vincula at the Tower of London.

Looking on from across the Channel, Francis I of France wrote a letter of commiseration to his English counterpart:

> *The lightness of women cannot bend the*
> *honour of men.*

To this day, Catherine's ghost is said to wander the Haunted Gallery at Hampton Court Palace, where she ran, screaming Henry's name, after being placed under house arrest, only to be dragged back by her guards.

THE VIRGIN QUEEN

Given the fate of her mother and various stepmothers, and having witnessed the sufferings of her half-sister, Mary, during a phantom pregnancy, not to mention the fact that a deadly epidemic of syphilis was raging across Europe at the time, it is probably not surprising that Elizabeth I vowed never to marry. Instead she pledged herself to her country, successfully ruling as Gloriana, Good Queen Bess, for almost forty-five years.

She was not without suitors, however, and also had special favourites among her courtiers, so it has long been asked whether Elizabeth really was the 'Virgin Queen' she claimed to be. The simplest answer is probably yes and no. Intelligent, lively, passionate and fun-loving, both as princess and queen, Elizabeth liked the company of men and was linked to several over her lifetime, including Thomas Seymour, Robert Dudley, Robert Devereux, Sir Walter Raleigh and Sir Christopher Hatton.

Rumours and speculation about her love life were rife and she probably did have lovers, although intimacy almost certainly stopped short of full intercourse. Fear of pregnancy alone would have dictated that, in addition to which Elizabeth was well aware she had to rule as if she were a king rather than as an attendant and subservient queen, the position to which she would have been relegated had she married.

The most important of Elizabeth's alleged lovers was Robert Dudley, who remained close to the queen until his death in 1588. They knew one another from childhood, were the same age and had been taught mathematics, riding and dancing together. They had even been imprisoned in the Tower together as traitors during Mary's reign.

On her accession to the throne following Mary's death in November 1558, Elizabeth made Dudley Master of the Horse, which meant she saw him almost daily; by many accounts the pair were openly flirtatious. Court gossip claimed they were lovers and certainly the mysterious salary of £500 that Elizabeth paid to Dudley's servant Tamworth suggests there was something to hide. But gossip aside, Dudley was no stranger to scandal, having married Amy Robsart when they were both seventeen and subsequently abandoned her in the country when he came to court. Both the Venetian and Spanish ambassadors expressed the opinion that Elizabeth was simply biding her time waiting for Dudley's wife to die, and rumours went into overdrive in 1560 when Amy was found lying at the foot of a staircase in their country house, her neck broken.

With so much gossip flying around court, marriage to Dudley would have been impossible, and Elizabeth was advised she would face open revolt from many of her close advisers if she so much as considered it. She in many ways distanced herself from Dudley after his wife's death, although she was always jealous of other women with whom he was associated and flew into a rage at news of his marriage to Lettice Devereux, her distant cousin, in 1579. Although Elizabeth never forgave Lettice, her attachment to Dudley continued. Not normally known for her generosity, she showered him with elaborate gifts and estates. She made him Protector of the Realm, with a vast salary, and also Earl of Leicester. In one of his final acts before his death, Dudley advised Elizabeth to don armour and address her troops as a strong, fearless monarch on the eve of the Spanish Armada in 1588.

On Elizabeth's death in 1603, a note from Dudley was found among her belongings. It was marked in her own handwriting as his last letter.

VIVE LA FRANCE: SETTING THE STANDARD FOR ROYAL MISTRESSES

There have been royal mistresses for as long as there have been kings, but one of the earliest about whom we know more than just her name – and of whom we even have surviving portraits – is fifteenth-century French courtesan Agnès Sorel.

Known as the *Dame de Beauté*, the Lady of Beauty, she was the first royal mistress to be officially recognized.

Agnès bore King Charles VII of France three daughters and is credited with rousing him from a long period of depression. In return he gave her wealth, land, chateaux and public acknowledgment. She wielded considerable influence at court and encouraged Charles to rally his troops and drive the English from French soil. It was to support this campaign that the heavily pregnant Agnès set out in midwinter from the Chateau of Chinon to join her husband in Jumièges in Normandy, where she died shortly after giving birth to her fourth child in February 1450.

There are several portraits of Agnès, best-known among them Jean Fouquet's painting of 1449, in which she is depicted as the Virgin Mary with one of her breasts completely exposed. The painting was displayed in a church and her detractors later commented that it was perhaps divine punishment that she died in childbirth not long afterwards. There is further controversy surrounding her death: whereas it was originally thought she had died from dysentery, scientists have now concluded the true cause was mercury poisoning. Either way, the grief-stricken king made Agnès a posthumous duchess and buried her with great pomp and ceremony.

MAÎTRESSE-EN-TITRE

It was another French king, Francis I, a contemporary of Henry VIII, who gave his favourite mistress the title *maîtresse-en-titre*, or official royal mistress.

Seigneur de Brantôme, the court gossip and raconteur, recorded a story about how the twenty-three-year-old Françoise de Foix was entertaining another lover when King Francis arrived unexpectedly. Afraid of being discovered, her lover, Admiral Bonnivet, quickly hid himself in the large fireplace. It was summer and the hearth was conveniently filled with scented pine branches, which provided excellent cover.

After enjoying himself thoroughly with Françoise, the king was desperately in need of a pee and relieved himself in the fireplace, unknowingly drenching his rival, the admiral.

Another story survives concerning Francis and one of his many mistresses. He arrived at her bedchamber only to find her husband armed with a sword. Not easily deterred, Francis warned the man that he would lose his head if he harmed his wife, booted him from the room and carried on regardless.

IN PRAISE OF OLDER WOMEN

Thanks to the elevated position of *maîtresse-en-titre*, French royal mistresses exerted more power than their counterparts anywhere else in Europe for almost two centuries, until Madame du Barry, former mistress of Louis XV, lost her head to the guillotine during the French Revolution in 1793.

Already an influence at the court of the sixteenth-century Francis I, Diane de Poitiers was to become the favoured mistress and lifelong companion of his son, King Henry II. She was thirty-five and he was sixteen when their union began. Politically astute and intelligent, she jointly signed official documents with the king as HenriDiane. She wielded considered influence, was a member of the privy council, appointed ministers and advised Henry in all matters. And when Henry jousted at tournaments, it was Diane's ribbon, not his wife's, that he carried on his lance.

Henry had married Catherine de Medici when they were both fourteen, but after nine years of marriage there was no heir. Diane knew this was sufficient cause for an annulment but had no wish for a more beautiful or assertive replacement, so she encouraged her lover to sleep with his wife regularly – even, so it's said, priming him for his conjugal duty. It worked: Henry and Catherine produced ten children.

Wanting to know the romantic secrets of her much older rival, Catherine was reported to have drilled a spyhole to watch Henry and Diane together. She was shocked to see Henry's tenderness with his lover. But Catherine was to have her revenge. When Henry was mortally wounded in a jousting accident in 1559, she took charge and barred Diane from seeing him as he lay dying, although he called out repeatedly for his mistress. After his death, Catherine banished Diane from the Château de Chenonceaux, which Henry had given her. Diane lived out her remaining years quietly in her Château d'Anet.

THE MERRY MONARCH

Living in exile during the years of Oliver Cromwell's Commonwealth, King Charles II of England spent his formative years at the French court, where the air of frivolity and decadence seems to have rubbed off.

Charles was a compulsive womanizer; he loved women and sex and sought to enjoy himself whenever and as much as possible. To celebrate his coronation in 1660, for example, Charles bedded his married mistress, Barbara Villiers, who nine months later gave birth to a daughter. Fortunately for all concerned, Barbara and her husband enjoyed what might be called an open marriage, and Charles even made him Earl of Castlemaine in recognition of his wife's services. Barbara, who was made Duchess of Cleveland, bore Charles five children in total, and she made sure all were acknowledged, legitimized and ennobled.

The tall, voluptuous redhead was one of the great beauties of her day, but Barbara was also extravagant, grasping, had a wicked temper and was wildly promiscuous. She was reported to take bribes and money from the privy purse and her influence made her unpopular, although Samuel Pepys was an admirer and wrote glowing reports of her physical attractiveness in his diaries.

Charles's great friend and favourite poet, the famously lewd Earl of Rochester, was responsible for coining the king's nickname in this verse:

> *Tho' Safety, Law, Religion, Life lay on't*
> *'Twould break through all to make its way to Cunt.*
> *Restless he rolls about from Whore to Whore*
> *A Merry Monarch, scandalous and poor!*

Charles happily bedded actresses and aristocrats, frolicking with whores or other men's wives without discrimination, although he did have a taste for the beautiful, clever and good-humoured. Under him many of Oliver Cromwell's strict

Puritan laws were repealed, and an air of louche celebration descended on the country, with the king's court at the centre of festivities. Incapable of fidelity to any one woman, Charles had a great many mistresses alongside Barbara Villiers, among them actress Nell Gwyn and her French rival Louise de Kérouaille, Duchess of Portsmouth, bisexual socialite Hortense Mancini, and possibly Frances Stewart, Duchess of Richmond, on whom the image of Britannia, which still features on some British coins, was based.

THE KING'S MATCH

Not least because of her husband's convenient absence, Barbara Villiers, Charles II's most formidable mistress, was in many ways his perfect bedmate. As voracious as the monarch when it came to sex, she was also fiercely ambitious – she even demanded he acknowledge her sixth child, although both knew very well that Charles was not the father. Those wanting access to the king quickly realized they would be wise to make Barbara an ally. Like her Parisian contemporary Madame de Montespan, mistress of Louis XIV, Barbara was one of the most powerful and influential figures at court for the thirteen years she held sway.

In 1662 she persuaded Charles to make her lady-in-waiting to his new queen, Catherine of Braganza: a great honour for Barbara, but a great shock for Queen Catherine, who knew of Barbara by reputation. When introduced to her husband's beautiful and haughty mistress she promptly collapsed with a nosebleed.

Barbara's taste for diversity matched Charles's own and on more than one occasion he surprised her entertaining another man. She developed a taste for younger working-class men, including her own servants, providing they were muscular and strong. By 1674, after a string of extra affairs, Barbara had moved to France, but Charles continued to pay her not inconsiderable gambling debts and she kept her full pension until her death in 1709.

Barbara Villiers, considered to be one of the most beautiful
Royalist women of her time

PRETTY, WITTY NELL GWYN

Nell Gwyn

Nell Gwyn was born in Coal Yard Alley off Drury Lane in London's Covent Garden, a rough area at the time. Her mother, known as Old Madam Gwyn, took to drinking heavily when Nell's father left; she ran a bawdy house, or brothel, to support her family. Young Nell served drinks to the customers and it's possible she even worked as a prostitute, either there or at nearby Madam Ross's house.

By thirteen, Nell was selling oranges at the Theatre Royal on Drury Lane with her sister Rose. Her pretty looks and quick-witted remarks soon caught the attention of the actors and she herself began acting. She was a talented comic actress and the riotous Restoration plays in which she often appeared dressed in tight breeches showed off her charms and physical assets; her first lover was the actor-manager Charles Hart. Samuel Pepys praised her performances and it was not long before she was invited to entertain royal parties.

Nell made Charles II laugh with her comic turns and sharp humour; despite Bishop Burnet commenting that she was 'the indiscreetest and wildest creature that ever was in court', she soon became the king's mistress. She called Charles her 'Charles the Third', since her two previous lovers had shared the same name, and he admired her liveliness and vivacity, but he was not as generous to her as he had been to other more aristocratic mistresses. Even after the birth of their son Charles in 1670, Nell continued to work as an actress, maybe as a dig at the king's shabby treatment of her. Charles took the hint and settled her in a townhouse in Pall Mall, bought her furniture and paid for her living expenses. She retired from the stage.

Nell knew how to get what she wanted and was not afraid of her competition.

She saw off Moll Davis, another actress whom Charles had been seeing. On one occasion, knowing her rival had an assignation with the king, Nell and her friend, the playwright Aphra Behn, slipped a hefty dose of laxative into Moll's afternoon cake, making absolutely sure she never made it to the king's bed that night. Nell was just as confident with Charles's duchesses. She teased Louise for her histrionics, calling her the 'weeping willow', and mocked her for her affectations. When Barbara Villiers drove her fine carriage and horses – a present from Charles – past Nell's house in an attempt to put the actress in her place, Nell responded the next day by driving a cart and oxen past the Duchess's house, shouting, 'Whores to market!'

Her most famous remark came while driving through Oxford in a coach. The crowd mistook her for the king's French Catholic mistress, Louise de Kérouaille, and began booing and jeering. Nell popped her head out, smiled broadly at the mob and cried, 'Good people, you are mistaken. I am the Protestant whore.'

Nell was perfectly happy with who she was, but did not see that the noble-born mistresses were any different. She was, however, furious when Charles gave Louise de Kérouaille three titles, including Duchess of Portsmouth, and berated him for treating her and their sons differently because she was a commoner. At the end of her tether during one visit by the king, Nell cried out to her son, 'Come hither, you little bastard! Say hello to your father.' Charles swiftly remedied the matter by making little Charles Earl of Burford and later Duke of St Albans, arranging an advantageous marriage for him with a wealthy heiress. Their younger son, James, became Lord Beauclerc, while Nell received the freehold of the house in Pall Mall as well as Burford House on the edge of Home Park, conveniently close to Windsor Castle.

There were always other mistresses but Charles remained close to Nell for the rest of his life, on his deathbed famously urging his brother, 'Let not poor Nelly starve.'

And Nell for her part remained faithful to her king. Whereas others had been guilty of blatant infidelity during his lifetime, Nell rejected any would-be suitors after Charles's death.

LOUISE DE KÉROUAILLE AND THE HOUSE OF WINDSOR

Born to noble but impoverished parents in Brittany in 1649, Louise was placed in the household of Henrietta Stuart, Duchess of Orléans, the youngest sister of Charles II. It was said that her family hoped she would become a royal mistress to Louis XIV. Instead she accompanied the Duchess of Orléans to England in 1670, and when Henrietta died suddenly Louise was made lady-in-waiting to Charles's queen, Catherine of Braganza.

Her rather innocent face hid a steely will and intelligence, and she only agreed to Charles's advances when she was absolutely certain of his affection for her. Her son Charles – the king's fourth illegitimate son of the same name – was born in 1672 and soon created Duke of Richmond.

Louise also received support from the French envoy on the understanding that she would serve her country's interests, and Louis XIV sent her lavishly extravagant gifts. This made her highly suspect in the eyes of the public and she was generally disliked. Nell Gwyn, her arch-rival for the king's affections, dubbed her 'Squintabella' and commented that her underclothes were not clean.

Nevertheless, Louise remained close to Charles. She thoroughly understood his character and this allowed her to keep her hold on him even through a long illness. She caught a virulent form of venereal disease from the king in 1674, whether syphilis or not is uncertain, but she recovered – although doctors warned her not to have sex with Charles again. It is a mark of his love for her that she remained his mistress with little or no sex from that time on. He affectionately called her Fubbs, meaning plump or chubby, and the royal yacht that was built in 1682 was named HMY *Fubbs*. On his deathbed, alongside good wishes for Nell Gwyn, Charles instructed his brother to 'do well by Portsmouth' (her title as duchess). Louise returned to Paris and lived to the grand old age of eighty-five. Rather intriguingly, her descendants include Diana, Princess of Wales, Camilla, Duchess of Cornwall, and Sarah, Duchess of York.

FLAMBOYANT, FABULOUS AND FASCINATING: THE REMARKABLE STORY OF HORTENSE MANCINI

One of the five celebrated Mancini sisters, Hortense was expected to attract a rich and titled husband when she arrived at the French court from Italy. Charles II was one of her many suitors but he was rejected by her influential uncle Cardinal Mazarin, chief minister of France, as lacking prospects. This was rather an error of judgement on the cardinal's part, as Charles was restored to the English throne a matter of months later.

In 1661, at the age of fifteen, Hortense was married to one of the richest men in Europe, Armand-Charles de la Porte, Duc de La Meilleraye. They became Duke and Duchess of Mazarin after their wedding.

A mismatch from the outset, the marriage was a disaster. The duke had some very strange ideas, even by the standards of the day; inspired by an odd mixture of insane jealousy and absurd morality, he exercised complete control over his household, including the servants. He had the front teeth of his female servants pulled out to make them less attractive and he stopped milkmaids from milking as he thought cows' udders had sexual connotations. He also painted over anything remotely suggestive or explicit in his extensive art collection.

Not surprisingly, the duke distrusted his ebullient young wife and forbade her from seeing any other men. He made frequent midnight searches for hidden lovers and forced her to spend hours every day at prayer. The final straw came when he insisted they move to the country. Shortly after, Hortense began a lesbian affair with Sidonie de Courcelles and was quickly dispatched to a convent for correction. This was not a success, as Sidonie was sent along with her, and the two indulged in a series of schoolgirl pranks at the nuns' expense before escaping up a chimney. Hortense's wild sense of fun never left her and it was one of the characteristics that later endeared her to Charles II.

Despite their obvious differences, the duke and duchess managed to produce four children before Hortense finally fled her tyrannical husband, running away on the night of 13 June 1668. She stayed with various relatives and even former suitors across Europe, reliant on their generosity as the duke controlled her finances and left her penniless. Finally, in 1675, Hortense travelled to London dressed as a man, ostensibly to visit her cousin, Mary of Modena, the new wife of Charles II's brother James, but her sights were set firmly on the king.

Dark-haired, exotic and wild, Hortense was ensconced in Charles's bed within a year, with a grand annual pension of £4,000. But rather like the Merry Monarch, she just couldn't help herself: London and the relaxed, decadent life of court suited her. The public tended to refer to her as the 'Italian whore' and she soon had a string of lovers.

Hortense's affair with Anne Lennard, Countess of Sussex, who was Charles's own daughter via Barbara Villiers, was scandalous even in relaxed Restoration England. When the pair were seen fencing in their nightgowns in St James's Park it proved the final straw for Anne's husband. He hauled her off to the country, where she took to her bed, weeping and kissing a miniature portrait of Hortense.

Not one to mourn for long, Hortense consoled herself by sleeping with Louis I de Grimaldi, Prince of Monaco. This was too much for Charles, who ended their affair but remained on friendly terms with her. According to diarist John Evelyn, just shortly before Charles's death he was 'sitting and toying with his concubines, Portsmouth, Cleveland, and Mazarin … Six days after, all was in dust.'

There were rumours that Hortense was romantically involved with the playwright Aphra Behn, who addressed the introduction of her *History of the Nun* to the Duchess of Mazarin:

> *To the Most Illustrious Princess, The Duchess of*
> *Mazarine … how infinitely one of Your own Sex ador'd*
> *You, and that, among all the numerous Conquest Your*

Grace has made over the Hearts of Men, Your Grace
had not subdu'd a more intire Slave ...

Hortense lived on in an elegant home in Chelsea, surrounding herself with witty, intellectual friends. After Charles's death she was supported financially first by his brother, James II, and then by William and Mary. She died at the age of fifty-three, possibly through suicide, although John Evelyn believed it was the result of heavy drinking. Never one to go quietly, in a bizarre twist her estranged husband claimed her body and insisted on taking it everywhere with him on his travels.

Anne, Countess of Sussex was to add to her own notoriety. Remaining unreconciled to her husband, she was taken to a nunnery in Paris in 1678, whereupon she swiftly made her escape. Still only seventeen, she embarked on a wild affair with the forty-year-old English ambassador, Ralph Montagu, who happened to be one of her mother's former lovers.

CHARLES'S CHILDREN

Charles acknowledged fourteen children with various mistresses and probably had several more besides. He and his wife had no children, however, which led to calls for an annulment to the marriage, so as to ensure a legitimate heir with a new bride. But Charles refused. He respected his wife and seems to have held her in some affection. He steadfastly maintained that the lack of an heir was not her fault.

A MISTRESS'S DUTY

While Charles was conducting his merry romps at the English court, Louis XIV was equally busy in France. The Sun King, architect of Versailles, had an insatiable libido. He was also extremely fertile. His official mistresses were constantly pregnant: Louise de la Vallière bore four children in seven years, while her successor, Athénaïs de Montespan, gave birth to seven in the space of nine years. When Louis married the ageing and virtuous Madame de Maintenon in 1685, she was long past childbearing and he was seventy-five, but nonetheless she had cause to complain to her priest that the king insisted upon sex at least once daily. The priest suggested it was her moral duty to comply, to prevent the king from sinning elsewhere.

Louis expected his mistresses never to be ill or too tired, and never to complain or be anything other than devoted to his happiness. They were expected to participate enthusiastically in all his hobbies and desires – after all, there was always someone willing and waiting to be next in line. The honour of travelling with him in the royal carriage was also a dubious one: Louis liked to eat a full meal en route, and his love of fresh air meant the windows would always be lowered, come rain or shine. And finally, however long the journey, nobody was allowed a loo break – or even to mention the subject.

LOVE POTIONS

Françoise Athénaïs de Montespan was cultured, charming and clever. With her thick golden hair, big blue eyes and cherubic lips, she also knew she was beautiful and was resolutely determined to replace Louise de la Vallière as King Louis XIV's official mistress. She made sure she was the confidante of both Louise and Queen Marie-Thérèse, and when both fell pregnant at the same time Madame de Montespan made her move. A formidable force, her temper tantrums were notorious, but she maintained her position and influence at court from 1667 until the scandal of the 'Affaire des Poisons' …

In 1679, fortune-teller and alleged witch Catherine Monvoisin, better known as La Voisin, was arrested in Paris. There had been a spate of suspicious deaths and La Voisin was accused of supplying potions and spells to both charm and poison. The real scandal, however, concerned her list of clients, which included many well-known society figures including Madame de Montespan.

It was alleged that Athénaïs had first visited La Voisin just before she replaced Louise de la Vallière in the king's affections, when the sorceress performed a black mass to cast a spell for her. After that, Madame de Montespan employed La Voisin whenever a problem arose in her relations with Louis, or whenever another mistress appeared on the scene. She was said to have regularly laced the king's food with a love potion provided by La Voisin and her associates. As the usual ingredients included animal teeth, bones and excrement, Spanish flies, human blood, dust and other remains, one can only imagine how repulsed the king must have felt when he recalled all the romantic meals he had shared with Athénaïs over the years.

Worse still, there were suggestions of a plot to poison him if he did not relinquish his latest young mistress, Angélique de Fontanges, followed by the final horror when the bodies of twenty-five infants were discovered buried in La Voisin's garden.

La Voisin was convicted of witchcraft and burned at the stake in February 1680. The names of her society clients were never publicly revealed; the court, fearing scandal and ridicule for the king, was at pains to conceal Madame de Montespan's association with a condemned murderer. So Athénaïs kept her apartment at Versailles but from that time on Louis XIV rarely visited her alone, and he certainly made sure never again to eat with her.

THE GOVERNESS WHO MARRIED A KING

After the pagan rituals of his last mistress were revealed, it is hardly surprising that Louis XIV should have a desire to cleanse his soul and look for more overtly Christian company. Even before the Affaire des Poisons, Louis appeared to tire of his long-time mistress. As Madame de Montespan's temper tantrums rose in tempo, the king spent an increasing amount of time with Madame de Maintenon.

When looking for a nurse and governess for her seven children with the king, Athénaïs de Montespan had been careful to choose a plain, sensible woman whom she considered unlikely to incite Louis's passions. The pious and sensible Madame de Maintenon seemed the perfect choice. For some years this worked, but Louis came to appreciate the love and attention the governess showed his children; he found her witty and intelligent and increasingly valued her opinions. At some point in the late 1670s the virtuous widow became arguably the first person to refuse Louis XIV anything when she declined to share his bed.

From then on, Louis was smitten and spent every spare moment in Madame de Maintenon's rooms, discussing politics, religion and art. Not long after the death of his queen, Marie-Thérèse, in 1683, Louis secretly married Madame de Maintenon. The difference in social status between them made an open marriage impossible and there was never any question of her becoming queen, but the ex-governess wielded considerable political influence over the king for the remainder of his reign.

THE BOY KING: LOUIS THE
WELL BELOVED

Louis XV succeeded his great-grandfather Louis XIV in 1715, at the age of five. He was married at fifteen to the twenty-two-year-old Polish princess Marie Leczinska, who was plain and dull but whose family were seen as reliably fertile. Marie did not disappoint, providing Louis with ten children in as many years.

Most unusually for a European monarch of the day, Louis was completely faithful to his wife for eight years. During that time he grew up into a notably handsome and attractive man, but despite his position he was less than confident and the boldly beautiful court ladies intimidated the shy king.

He finally chose as his mistress Louise-Julie de Mailly-Nesle, another plain but sweet-natured woman who remained his *maîtresse-en-titre* for seven years. Granddaughter of Hortense Mancini, she had four younger sisters, all more attractive and more conniving than she, and three of them succeeded her as Louis's mistress, each ousting the former with little show of conscience. But on the death of Marie-Anne, Duchesse de Châteauroux, the last of the Mailly sisters, the position of royal mistress was once again vacant.

Louis's gaze fell upon the twenty-four-year-old Jeanne-Antoinette d'Etiolles, a member of the Parisian bourgeoisie. Married with two small children, she was much celebrated for her fashionable salon, at which noted writers and philosophers would gather.

To become the official royal mistress and live at Versailles, however, Jeanne-Antoinette had to be ennobled and presented at court. Louis made her the Marquise de Pompadour and she duly appeared before the king and queen. The queen treated the new mistress kindly and she in return never failed to be respectfully considerate of her royal lover's wife.

Over the next nineteen years, Madame de Pompadour came to epitomize the idea of a French king's mistress.

Madame de Pompadour

A MODEL MISTRESS

After seven or eight years, alas, Madame de Pompadour's glowing looks began to fade, and following two miscarriages she also found herself less and less interested in sex. As she increasingly despaired of providing Louis with the child she longed to give him, so her libido dwindled until it was virtually non-existent.

Madame de Pompadour was desperate to hold on to her position and feared the arrival of another, more passionate, royal mistress. She met the king's every other need and kept him well entertained, and so, to satisfy his physical demands, she established what was in effect a discreet private brothel on the edge of Versailles. The Parc-aux-Cerfs (Stag Park) was designed for the king's pleasure: there, a couple of pretty girls plucked from the streets of Paris would stay, who were no threat to Madame de Pompadour, either intellectually or culturally. The arrangement was a success. Only one of the girls, the unlikely named Louise O'Murphy, attempted to create a division between the king and his official mistress; Louis was horrified and Madame de Pompadour had the young Louise hastily married with a large dowry shortly before she gave birth to the king's child.

Madame de Pompadour learned the lessons of previous royal mistresses and was rightly wary of rivals. She took care to be the perfect companion, discussing business, diplomacy, and hunting with Louis. Always plagued by poor health, she was at pains to hide any signs of this from the king, who had a horror of sickness.

Unlike other mistresses, and in stark contrast to her successor Madame du Barry, Madame de Pompadour preferred estates to jewels. In fact she twice handed back her jewels to the treasury to help out in times of war. Altogether she owned seventeen estates, plus houses she bought as an investment. She was accomplished and known for her good taste; over the years she spent a fortune improving and decorating her properties for the king's pleasure and convenience. She seems to have been a shrewd businesswoman, too, and ran and sold her estates at a profit. She gained popularity as a generous benefactor to charities and hospitals.

Louis XIV had never allowed his mistresses any political power – apart from Madame de Maintenon at the very end of his reign – while in England Charles II had been more easily influenced by the women in his life; particularly in his latter years he had been only too happy to leave affairs of state in the capable hands of Louise de Kérouaille while he romped with Nell Gwyn. But Madame de Pompadour undoubtedly wielded the greatest power of any European royal mistress. She knew she would need important, well-placed friends if she was to survive at court, and from the outset she used her influence to dismiss her enemies. She soon controlled all titles, honours and positions at court and, although her sexual relations with Louis XV dwindled, the two became even closer. The king moved her into palatial apartments directly above his own and saw her constantly.

In 1753, the Marquis d'Argenson referred to Madame de Pompadour as the unofficial prime minister of France, and indeed her instincts were usually sound – although she did encourage Louis to turn against France's traditional ally, Prussia, in the Seven Years' War in the late 1750s and early 1760s. The conflict ended fairly disastrously for France, which had to forfeit its American colonies to Britain and was left almost bankrupt. Madame de Pompadour consoled Louis with the now immortal phrase, 'Après nous, le déluge': after us, the flood – or, to paraphrase, it won't matter once we're dead and gone.

Madame de Pompadour remained Louis's official royal mistress until she died from tuberculosis in 1746 at the age of forty-two.

EMPRESS CATHERINE THE GREAT

Catherine the Great in 1762

No look at royal shenanigans would be complete without Catherine the Great, rumoured to be the most rampant royal of them all. In comparison with many of her male counterparts, Catherine clocked up a fairly modest twelve known lovers in forty years.

In her accession and rule, particularly after the assassination of her husband Peter III, she relied on her noble favourites, most notably Count Grigory Orlov and Grigori Potemkin. Both became her lovers but the real love of her life seems to have been Potemkin, who became her chief minister and adviser.

They exchanged a series of lovingly frank letters. In 1774, for instance, she wrote to him: 'My dear little pigeon, I love you very much; you are handsome, intelligent, amusing. I forget the entire world when I'm with you.'

Their affair ended in 1776 but they remained close and, in later years, Potemkin would introduce the empress to handsome young men. She was particularly partial to virile cavalry officers from the Imperial Horse Guard, and in this respect perhaps deserves her reputation. She developed a system whereby one of her close confidantes, Countess Bruce or Mademoiselle Protassov, would act as 'taster' for the empress, testing the sexual skills of the chosen officer. If they passed, Catherine would welcome them to her bed, showering them with money, property and servants for the year or so they remained her favourite. Her final lover was twenty-one-year-old Prince Plato Zubov. Catherine was in her sixties. It is likely that her sexual independence led to many of the wilder stories about her.

And what of the supposed sex with a stallion that crushed her to death, the one story that everyone seems to know? The truth is far more ordinary. Catherine died of a stroke while making her way to her water closet in 1796.

THE ULTIMATE ACCESSORY

Just as French was the language of court in many countries across Europe, so French tastes in fashion, style, art and architecture dominated from the Middle Ages. If an official royal mistress was de rigueur in Paris, then an official royal mistress was deemed essential for any reigning monarch who wanted to be taken seriously.

This was true across the continent, although for some of the German princes it seemed more a matter of form than practice. At the beginning of the eighteenth century, the elector of Brandenburg, Frederick III, had a suitably beautiful and aristocratic mistress who was well rewarded with gifts of jewellery. Frederick was appalled by the notion of adultery, however, and loved his wife far too much ever to be unfaithful to her.

When the elector of Hanover became George I of Great Britain in 1714, he brought two royal mistresses with him to court. But they failed to impress and became the subject of great ridicule, as one was short and fat, the other tall and thin, and both were considered ugly.

A FOOT FETISH

Ludwig I of Bavaria, a German prince of the early nineteenth century, provided one of the more bizarre tales of royal romance. While his wife frequently appeared in the same old dresses, he lavished jewels on his mistress, the Irish dancer Lola Montez. He also had an unhealthy obsession with her feet.

Several letters between the two survive which detail his fetish. In one, he writes, 'I want to take your feet in my mouth, at once, without giving you time to wash them after you've arrived from a trip.' There's more than a suggestion that Ludwig masturbated while sucking on Lola's toes and it seems this often occurred in place of intercourse, which they had infrequently.

Ludwig also liked Lola to wear squares of material about her body – it's not specified where. She would then give him the material and he liked to know exactly which side had been next to her skin so that he could place it against his. Later, while she was in exile, having fled at the start of the revolutions of 1848, he asked her to send him these materials.

THE SPANISH WAY

Impervious to French fashions or what went on in other European courts, royal mistresses in Spain were not well rewarded for their endeavours in the royal bedchamber. Perhaps out of consideration for their souls, when their time as favourite was over they were usually promptly packed off to a convent.

In the early 1700s, King John V of neighbouring Portugal cut out the middle man, so to speak, by recruiting his mistresses from the nuns at a Lisbon convent. The institution conveniently provided a nursery for any illegitimate royal offspring, and his son with the mother superior was later appointed archbishop.

PRINNY

George IV of England, nicknamed 'Prinny' in his long rule as Prince Regent during his father George III's repeated bouts of madness, entertained a string of mistresses; one of them, Mrs Fitzherbert, he even went so far as to marry, although their union was declared illegal under the terms of the Royal Marriages Act. Finally, drastically in debt and under pressure from his father and parliament, George agreed to marry the wealthy Princess Caroline of Brunswick.

Although rather too fond of food and with an already expanding waistline, George was a man of taste, inextricably bound up with Regency style, fastidious in his habits and a member of the beau monde. Caroline was a good-natured sort of girl, keen on horses and animals, but completely unaware of the need for personal hygiene or grooming, and the polar opposite of the dandy prince. The two were not destined to get along.

When George first saw his bride-to-be, he called for spirits and whispered that he was unwell. Caroline was also disappointed.

She had been expecting the virile young man in the portrait she had seen, not the plump fop with whom she was presented.

Nevertheless, George did his duty, spending the first two nights of their marriage in his wife's bed. Afterwards he wrote, 'She showed ... such marks of filth both in the fore and hind part of her ... that she turned my stomach and from that moment I made a vow never to touch her again.'

He was as good as his word and never did. Caroline was already pregnant and nine months later, in 1796, Princess Charlotte was born. George and Caroline were never to live together again, however; he even banned her from his coronation and tried to divorce her on the grounds of her infidelity. Princess Caroline retained the support of the public, though, while George was increasingly unpopular for his extravagance and dissolute lifestyle.

George remained close to Maria Fitzherbert throughout his life, although he was linked to several other women and fathered a number of illegitimate children. He had a habit of taking snuff from the ample cleavage of his mistress Lady Conyngham, while her husband sat placidly next to them, compensated no doubt by thoughts of the ample riches that were coming his way.

JEALOUS MONARCHS

Most monarchs seemed remarkably forgiving of their mistresses' peccadilloes. Maybe they saw it as the price to be paid for a lusty lover, or perhaps they were just realistic in light of their own lack of fidelity.

Peter the Great was less relaxed. Although he was himself an enthusiastic participator in drunken orgies, when he discovered that Anna Mons, his mistress of thirteen years, had taken the Swedish ambassador as her lover in 1703, he threw her in prison together with thirty of her friends.

JEALOUS WIVES

Catherine of Braganza was reluctantly forced to accept her husband Charles II's mistresses. And for the most part she made the best of things and got along with them. She must, however, have taken a secret satisfaction when she forced Barbara Villiers to ride horseback in a royal procession just two days after giving birth to yet another of Charles's illegitimate babies.

The Empress Eugenie, wife of Napoleon III of France, was incensed when his young seventeen-year-old mistress arrived at a ball barefoot, wearing a diaphanous, transparent gown with absolutely nothing on beneath it. Male courtiers were said to be entranced, their wives and other women present less so. The empress ordered Virginie di Castiglione to leave and not return unless she was more properly clothed.

Virginie lasted only a year as mistress. Self-absorbed and not very bright, she may have looked beautiful but the emperor soon found her boring.

THE PLAYBOY PRINCE, EDWARD VII

With the arrival at court of Queen Victoria's son, the future Edward VII, the British monarchy had found a rightful heir to Charles II's appetite and joie de vivre. Although it had been quite acceptable for Charles to be open about his amours during the debauched excesses of the later seventeenth century, the strictures of the Victorian age and the freedoms of the press meant that Edward had to uphold an appearance of discretion. This he managed surprisingly well, given the number of liaisons he enjoyed, and the majority of people believed his frequent female companions were 'just good friends'. And what a friendly prince he was.

Edward's playboy reputation stems from a stint with the army, on manoeuvres in Ireland in 1861. His fellow officers smuggled a would-be actress called Nellie Clifden into the young Prince of Wales's tent and she proceeded to open his eyes to a whole new world of experiences. Unfortunately for the prince, his parents found out and were horrified. Already ill at the time, an appalled Prince Albert travelled to see his son at Cambridge University to give him a stern lecture about morals. This had little effect on Edward, alas, but Albert became gravely ill and died shortly afterwards. Victoria went into a deep depression and extended mourning, blaming her son for his father's death.

On 10 March 1863, twenty-one-year-old Edward married eighteen-year-old Princess Alexandra of Denmark in St George's Chapel at Windsor Castle. They were a well-suited couple – the marriage was happy and they had six children together – but the die had been cast and Edward could not remain a one-woman man. His first official mistress was the flame-haired actress Lillie Langtry, and he subsequently included Daisy Greville, Countess of Warwick, the actress Sarah Bernhardt, Lady Randolph Churchill – mother of Winston – and Alice Keppel, the great-grandmother of Camilla, Duchess of Cornwall, among his lovers. He was rumoured to have had at least fifty-five liaisons of various degrees of intensity. Although most people remained oblivious, his affairs were the subject of society gossip and considerable newspaper speculation.

ABDICATION CRISIS

Edward VII was the first monarch to have to face the fact that times had changed. Unlike his predecessors, he could no longer parade his mistresses at court and expect his subjects and the nation's journalists not to intrude; an increasingly confident press was waiting at the ready to expose any indiscretion to a prurient public.

By the time his grandson Edward VIII came to power in 1936 there was no leeway at all where romantic scandal was concerned. When the king determined that he wished to marry his lover, the American double-divorcee Wallis Simpson, parliament gave him a simple ultimatum: either he renounce her or he renounce the throne.

The king followed his heart rather than his head, abdicating in favour of his brother, George VI – whose unimpressed wife, the future Queen Mother, would only refer to Mrs Simpson as 'that woman'. In his farewell address to the empire in December 1936, the outgoing monarch spoke honestly and openly about his beloved Wallis:

> *You all know the reasons which have impelled me to renounce the throne ... But you must believe me when I tell you that I have found it impossible to carry the heavy burden of responsibility and to discharge my duties as King as I would wish to do without the help and support of the woman I love.*

Edward and Wallis, now Duke and Duchess of Windsor, moved to France where they remained until his death in 1972. Wallis died in 1986.

PERVERSE PLEASURES

It's just human. We all have the jungle inside of us.
Diane Frolov & Andrew Schneider
Northern Exposure

Alongside the rules and regulations of accepted morality and immorality, or perhaps because of them, there were always those who liked to push the boundaries, to go just that little bit further to experience that extra excitement. In many cases it was harmless, no more daring than a secret, saucy tattoo or the thrill of illicit erotic literature. Sometimes, however, predilections slipped into a more dangerous world of perversity.

When the actor and playwright David Garrick asked the distinguished man of letters Samuel Johnson what he considered to be the two most important things in life, the great man did not hesitate in replying, 'Drinking and fucking'. However, Johnson also said, 'No people can be great who have ceased to be virtuous', and he was always at pains to control his more earthy instincts, believing a moral code of behaviour to be an imperative.

THE MARQUIS DE SADE

A fanciful portrait of the Marquis de Sade (1886)

Apparently unconcerned with any notions of self-control, the Marquis de Sade is inextricably associated with cruelty and sexual torture. Indeed the word sadism is taken from his name.

His notoriety stems from three main incidents – the whipping and imprisonment of Rose Keller, the Spanish Fly poisoning and the alleged kidnapping of a number of virgins, along with a series of complaints of sexual cruelty and perversion from a number of prostitutes and servants. Plus the novels he wrote in prison. The depraved tales of sexual deviance cemented his infamous reputation.

The Rose Keller scandal took place on Easter Sunday 1763.

Whether she was a prostitute or not has been a matter of debate, but de Sade persuaded Rose Keller to accompany him to his chateau at Arcueil near Paris. There he was said to have tied her up before whipping and slashing her skin, after which he dressed her wounds with ointment and put her to bed. Rose used the sheets to escape from a second-floor window. De Sade maintained this was valuable research to find a healing salve for wounds but he spent seven months in prison for the crime.

Forced into an arranged marriage in 1763 at the age of twenty-three, de Sade was in love with his wife's younger sister, Anne-Prospère, who he begged to be allowed to marry. Both his father and his mother-in-law forbade the match. Later, in 1772, Anne-Prospère went to live with de Sade at his chateau at Lacoste in Provence. It was during this time that the infamous 'poisoning' took place in Marseille.

At a ball, guests were served chocolate bonbons, so delicious that many people ate a great number of them. What they did not know was that de Sade had laced them with copious quantities of powdered Spanish Fly or cantharis beetle, a known aphrodisiac. A fevered orgy was said to have followed. Unfortunately, in high doses Spanish Fly was poisonous and many people fell ill, although no one died.

De Sade was accused of poisoning and sodomy with his manservant Latour, and the pair were sentenced to death in their absence. They fled to Italy with Anne-Prospère, who became ill after a few months there and died. After this de Sade seems to have returned to his wife, Renée-Pelagie, and remained in hiding at Lacoste. With the help of a good lawyer he stayed out of prison for the most part and over the next few years a number of servant girls were hired to work at the chateau; most left quickly complaining of their cruel mistreatment, to be replaced by others.

In 1777, the Marquis de Sade was tricked into returning to Paris where, largely due to the efforts of his mother-in-law, Madame de Montreuil, he was imprisoned in the Chateau de Vincennes. He was to spend a great deal of the next thirty-seven years incarcerated and it was while there that he began writing his pornographic novels, including *Justine, ou les malheurs de la vertu* (the misfortunes of virtue) and *Juliette, ou les prospérités du vice* (the fortunes of vice). The novels told the stories of two sisters: the virtuous Justine, who was subjected to every conceivable twisted depravity and torture, and Juliette, who revelled in vice but lived a happy, carefree, prosperous life.

It was while he was in Vincennes that de Sade was accused of kidnapping and murdering a number of virgins. This he always denied, accounting for the whereabouts of each girl. He wrote to his wife in 1781 defending himself, saying, 'Yes, I admit that I am a libertine; I have devised everything that can be done in that line, but I have not practised all that I have devised and I never intend to do so. I may be a libertine, but I am neither a criminal nor a murderer . . .' He signed the letter in blood.

He appealed his death sentence but remained in prison, transferring to the Bastille when Vincennes was closed. He was moved to the insane asylum at Charentes after shouting out to passers-by about the sexual habits of the prison governor.

NEW WORLD PERVERSITY

When looking for crimes and misdemeanours, including sexual misadventures, court records are always useful sources; whether a sin against the morals of the time or a real crime, they detail every case. When the Pilgrim Fathers sailed the *Mayflower* into Plymouth Bay in December 1620, William Bradford kept a detailed journal of the life of the new settlement. As Governor of Plymouth Colony from 1621 he was in a good position to know exactly what went on.

Governor Bradford wrote *Of Plymouth Plantation* as a detailed two-volume history. A narrow population, hunger, harsh conditions and disease all exacerbated the normal problems of people living in close proximity and meant he regularly had to deal with a wide range of moral and marital issues. Depending on the offence, often the harshest of punishments were meted out. One of the saddest occurred in 1642.

A sixteen-year-old youth named Thomas Granger was caught *in flagrante* with a mare. Bradford records, 'He was this year detected of buggery, and indicted for the same, with a mare, a cow, two goats, five sheep, two calves, and a turkey. Horrible it is to mention but the truth of the history requires it.'

Upon questioning poor Granger admitted that he was guilty several times over with the mare and all the other animals, confirming the fact to court and jury. He then identified each of the animals in turn, which was easy apart from the sheep when it appears he had some difficulty telling one from another. This would be comedic if he had not been executed for the sin, as were all the animals: 'The cattle were all cast into a great and large pit that was digged of purpose for them and no use made of any part of them.'

Bradford's records suggest such cases were not as unusual as might be supposed. Another governor of the New Haven Colony, Theophilus Eaton, wrote of a similar case where a man called Thomas Hogg was accused of fathering a piglet with a sow. Impossible though that seems, the remarkable resemblance of piglet to man was taken as certain evidence; both had a similarly lazy right eye. In the event, Hogg was let off lightly with a whipping and hard labour in prison to cure him of his lusts. History does not reveal what happened to the piglet.

THE HELLFIRE CLUB

At a time when establishment gentlemen's clubs catered for every interest, the original Hellfire Club was set up by Philip Duke of Wharton in 1719 as a satirical version. The intention was to ridicule religion and morality and to shock society, but it was meant as more of a joke than a serious attack. The president was referred to as the Devil and members as devils, hence the name, but there is no evidence of any satanic worship or belief. Wharton himself was on the one hand a prominent, well-educated politician, and on the other a drunk, a libertine, and a rake.

The club met on Sundays, often at The Greyhound Tavern,

but since women were admitted as well as men, unlike other clubs of the time, meetings were also held at members' houses, as women could not be seen in taverns. The club closed in 1721 when George I, influenced by Robert Walpole, put forward the 'Bill against Immorality' which was primarily aimed at the Hellfire Club. Wharton went on to become a Freemason and Grand Master of England.

Francis Dashwood and the Earl of Sandwich are alleged to have been members of a Hellfire Club in the 1730s that met at the George and Vulture tavern in Cornhill in London. Dashwood then founded the Order of the Knights of St Francis in 1746. The meetings were so popular that the tavern proved too small and proceedings moved to Dashwood's country house at West Wycombe, first gathering there on 1 May, Walpurgis Night, 1752. This choice of date and festival reflected Dashwood's obsession with paganism.

Thereafter Dashwood leased Medmenham Abbey, a Tudor mansion on the banks of the Thames near Marlowe in Buckinghamshire, that had originally been a Cistercian abbey. There was a cave beneath the abbey which Dashwood believed to be an old heathen site, and he excavated a series of further caves where the Hellfire club could celebrate their rites. Members by now included many of the most influential figures of the day, including John Montagu the Fourth Earl of Sandwich, Robert Vansittart, who went on to become Governor of Bengal, Thomas Potter, MP and son of the Archbishop of Canterbury, John Wilkes, radical MP and journalist, and Benjamin Franklin, later one of the Founding Fathers of America. The artist William Hogarth was also associated with the club and he painted a portrait of Dashwood as St Francis.

The meetings were the subject of much speculation, and rumours of debauchery, pagan orgies, sacrifice and black masses were rife at the time. It is hard to separate fact from fiction but members supposedly wore ritual white clothing while Dashwood as 'abbott' wore red. The caves were said to be decorated with mythological images of Venus, Bacchus and Priapus, along with phalluses and other sexual themes, though none of these survive. Dashwood's mistress, a well-known London madam referred to as 'Hellfire Stanhope', and several of her molls would travel down to take part in the rites. These female guests were euphemistically called 'nuns' and the meetings were most likely nothing more than an excuse for a weekend of revelry, drinking, feasting and sex.

In 1762, Francis Dashwood was appointed Chancellor of the Exchequer, although he was forced to resign the following year when his tax on cider almost caused riots. After that he took up his seat in the House of Lords as the fifteenth Baron Le Despencer. The meetings dwindled and by 1766 the Hellfire Club was no more.

DEATH BY MISADVENTURE

In an echo of the excesses of some late twentieth-century musicians, Franz Kotzwara was a celebrated Czech double bass player and composer with a taste for high living, women and drunken, kinky sex. He lived a nomadic existence, travelling around Europe performing with different orchestras, but in late summer 1791 he was in London.

On the evening of 2 September, he visited Susannah Hill, a prostitute in Vine Street, Piccadilly. After they had eaten dinner he offered her two shillings and demanded that she cut off his testicles. She refused, but he then fastened a rope ligature around his neck which he tied to a door knob and strangled himself whilst having sex with Susannah.

A sensational trial at the Old Bailey followed in which Susannah Hill was accused of murder. Luckily for the girl, there were sufficient witnesses and evidence for Kotzwara's particular sexual proclivities for the prostitute to be acquitted.

Court records were destroyed in a bid to avoid a scandal, although it seems that a copy was made and a graphically detailed pamphlet produced. It was probably the first documented death from auto-erotic asphyxiation.

MAD, BAD, AND DANGEROUS TO KNOW

Born in 1788, George Gordon Byron was a renowned poet and leading figure in the Romantic movement. He epitomized aristocratic excess and ran up huge debts, but he was notorious for his torrid love affairs and scandalous rumours of an incestuous relationship.

Educated at Harrow School and Trinity College Cambridge, Byron was over-indulged by his doting mother. He always lacked discipline and was passionate by nature. He wrote, 'My school friendships were with me passions (for I was always violent).'

His Grand Tour was diverted to the Mediterranean and Levant as most of Europe was out of bounds due to Napoleon's campaigns. It was on Byron's return that he began the first of a number of affairs. Dazzling, brilliant, dark and brooding, it is little wonder that Lady Caroline Lamb gave him the epithet 'mad, bad and dangerous to know'. At first she dismissed him, but the two soon became lovers and caused a society scandal. Caroline Lamb was married to Lord Melbourne, who later became British Prime Minister, and she was obsessed with Byron, famously dressing as a boy wearing a page's clothes to run alongside his coach.

Byron tired of the relationship and moved quickly on, although Caroline Lamb never fully recovered, especially as Byron was to marry her cousin, Anne Isabella Milbanke. Byron and Anne had a daughter, Augusta Ada, but the marriage was not happy. Byron treated Anne unkindly and rumours persisted of an incestuous affair with Augusta Leigh, his half-sister. The two had seen little of one another as children growing up but formed a close bond as adults. There were other damaging suggestions of violence and sodomy. Seemingly unable to avoid a scandal, Byron left England in 1816, never to return.

That summer he lived in Italy in the Villa Diodati with Percy Bysshe Shelley, Shelley's future wife Mary Godwin, and her cousin Claire Clairmont. Trapped inside the villa by weeks of rain, the intense atmosphere there inspired Mary Shelley to create the story that was to become *Frankenstein*.

Byron died of fever in Missolonghi in 1824. Aged thirty-six he had travelled to Greece to fight for freedom against the oppressive Ottoman Empire.

VICTORIA AND ALBERT

Queen Victoria and her consort Prince Albert of Saxe-Coburg, those upholders of morality who set the standard for Victorian values for ever more, obviously had an active sex life. Couples don't tend to have nine children without a healthy dose of lust mixed in with the love and affection, even royal couples in the nineteenth century. But there are a couple of surprising twists.

There are persistent rumours that Victoria had a small tattoo 'intimately' placed, so not on general display. As it is said to depict a Bengal tiger fighting a python, a suitably feisty and powerful image, one has to wonder quite how small or discreet it could really have been.

Prince Albert has a very particular form of permanent piercing, or ringing, named after him. In the nineteenth century, the vogue was for men to wear very tight breeches. To avoid unsightly bulges the penis was pierced through the urethra and a ring inserted. A ribbon could then be slipped through the ring to anchor the member tidily to the inseam of the breeches. It was claimed that Prince Albert's ring also helped to hold back his uncircumcised foreskin to improve personal hygiene.

TATTOOS

George 'Professor' Burchett, the 'King of Tattooists', who was expelled from school in 1884 at the age of twelve for tattooing his classmates, never claimed Queen Vic amongst his royal clients. He did however tattoo her grandson King George V, King Frederick IX of Denmark, and King Alphonso XIII of Spain among his many clients and reflected in his memoirs that following the queen's death on 22 January 1901, he had to work day and night for weeks to keep up with the demand for commemorative tattoos saying, 'In Memory of Our Queen'.

The history of tattoos stretches back to the earliest days of mankind. The two oldest colour tattoos were found on a Stone Age man who died over 5,000 years ago and an ancient Egyptian priestess of the goddess Hathor dating back over four thousand years. Tattoos were well known in ancient Greece, although they were usually associated with slaves, and it is sometimes claimed that Anglo-Saxon kings were tattooed.

There was sometimes a sexual significance to tattoos, particularly amongst tribal groups where they were used to boost fertility and as a charm to guard against sterility. Behaviourist and psychologist Havelock Ellis, who wrote *Studies in the Psychology of Sex* in the early twentieth century, included tattoo fetishists. One man, after having a butterfly tattooed on his penis, reported, 'I experienced a few minutes after leaving the shop, the phenomena of erection and ejaculation accompanied by a feeling of physical exaltation so great that it almost prostrated me afterwards.'

Picts (*c.* 300 BC) covered in body art

The voyages of discovery are credited with reintroducing tattooing to Europe. Sir Martin Frobisher returned from an expedition in search of the North-West Passage with three Inuits, a man, woman and child, who proved a great attraction at the court of Queen Elizabeth I, particularly as the woman had tattoos on her chin and forehead.

The word tattoo comes from the Tahitian *tatau* and it was only after Cook's botanist Sir Joseph Banks and several sailors returned from the voyages to the South Pacific sporting tattoos that the idea caught on and tattooists began working, especially in sea ports.

By the nineteenth century, led by monarchs and heads of state, tattoos were popular amongst the upper classes throughout Europe. Winston Churchill's mother, Jennie, Lady Randolph Churchill, had a snake tattooed around her wrist which she would cover with a specially designed diamond bracelet whenever the occasion demanded. Churchill himself had an anchor tattooed on his forearm.

VICTORIAN PORNOGRAPHY

According to the Oxford English Dictionary, the word pornography was first used around 1850 and it literally means writings about or by prostitutes or *pornoi*. Such writings obviously existed long before, you only have to remember Aretino's work in Renaissance Italy. The Obscene Publications Act of 1857 tightened the law and literary censorship in Britain, allowing magistrates to order the destruction of anything considered licentious – 'any obscene publication held for sale or distribution'. This covered books, prints and leaflets. In effect, the act served to increase the market for smuggled French pornography, for which there appeared to be an insatiable demand.

AN ENGLISHMAN IN PARIS

Frederick Hankey, a military captain with a particular taste for decadence, moved to Paris upon his retirement in pursuit of pleasure. He was only too willing to supply titillating tracts and Gallic erotica for an eager British clientele.

Hankey by all accounts was a fairly unpleasant character. Even his friend, the Victorian collector of pornography Henry Spencer Ashbee, commented that he was 'a second Sade without the intellect'.

Writers and critics, the brothers Edmond and Jules de Goncourt, meeting him in Paris in 1862, described him in less than flattering terms: 'He is a young man of about thirty years old, his temples puffed out like an orange, his eyes of a clear and piercing blue, his skin extremely thin and revealing the sub-cutaneous networks of veins . . .' They further deplored his perverted tastes, calling him 'a madman, a monster, one of those men who linger in the abyss . . . a man who enjoys his libertinage only through the suffering of women.'

The brothers also refer to Hankey's grotesque commission to the explorer Sir Richard Burton for the skin of a woman from his travels in Africa. Hankey seems to have wanted it for the cover and binding of some books. Burton did not fufil the request.

As well as publishing pornography to smuggle back to England, Hankey had his own sizeable collection of sadomasochistic material which he left to Henry Spencer Ashbee on his death in 1882.

HENRY SPENCER ASHBEE

Ashbee was a book lover, writer and traveller, and the major Victorian collector of pornography. He amassed thousands of volumes in a number of different languages. He was also the author, under the pseudonym Pisanus Fraxi, of a comprehensive three-volume survey of the subject.

When he died in 1900, he bequeathed the entire collection of 15,299 pornography books to the British Museum. The museum authorities were extremely reluctant to take it, but alongside the erotica they would also receive Ashbee's unique collection of Cervantes' *Don Quixote* editions and translations. He had effectively blackmailed the British Museum into accepting his erotic literature, ensuring the collection, his life's work, would remain intact.

THE ENGLISH VICE

From the eighteenth century, those interested in the erotic possibilities of flogging read Edmund Curll's translation from Latin of the German physician Johann Heinrich Meibom's 1639 work *A Treatise on the Use of Flogging*.

It was incredibly influential at the time, giving a detailed physiological explanation for the effects of beating and flogging, with references to classical writings to support his theories. He explained, 'There are Persons who are stimulated to Venery by

Strokes of Rods, and worked up into a Flame of Lust by Blows, and that Part, which distinguishes us to be Men, should be raised by the Charm of Invigorating Lashes.'

The idea of whipping for sexual pleasure came to be nicknamed 'the English vice'. Fostered by the often brutal corporal punishments meted out at public school, it was particularly popular with the upper classes and men of high office. The details might vary but the basic scenario was that the man (or occasionally woman) misbehaved and was flogged or spanked as punishment.

The black market for flagellant pornography thrived in Victorian Britain and thousands of books and pamphlets on the subject were produced or smuggled in to the country. Alongside the literature, a number of brothels catered specifically for those with a taste for pain. One of the most popular was run by Mrs Theresa Berkley at number 28 Charlotte Street in the heart of London's Fitzrovia. There she not only meted out the punishments, but had a number of girls who were themselves willing to be flogged if that happened to be the gentleman's pleasure, amongst them Mary Wilson writing *Venus Schoolmistress* in 1877 listed: 'Miss Ring, Hannah Jones, Sally Taylor, One-Eyed Peg, Bauld-cunted Poll, and a black girl called Ebony Bet.' The 'Berkeley Horse', which looked like two ladders forming an upside-down 'V', was developed to help with the flogging.

So successful was Mrs Berkley as a dominatrix, that when she died she left her brother over £10,000, a small fortune worth almost a million pounds today. As a devout missionary, he felt it his duty to refuse the legacy.

THE LIBERAL VICTORIAN

Henry Havelock Ellis was a British doctor, writer, social reformer and pioneer researcher into sexual behaviour. A liberal idealist, he was one of the first people to openly support homosexuals' rights as well as women's rights to birth control.

Ellis had his own particular predilection. As a boy, he had visited London Zoo with his mother and without her meaning him to, he happened to see her urinate on the ground. As an adult he came to associate the act with feelings of affection and warmth for women. He liked to watch his lovers' 'golden showers', which he saw as the inspiration for fountains. He also believed that Rembrandt had depicted this in a painting of 1654 but the stream of urine had been painted out. He undertook a number of scientific studies of women's urine streams which were published in the *American Journal of Dermatology* in 1902.

THE TRUTH ABOUT VAN GOGH'S EAR

He is remembered as the tortured genius who cut off his own ear for love as he struggled with depression and bouts of mental illness. The truth may be more complex.

Van Gogh was wracked by sexual jealously. Living in Arles in southern France where the women had a reputation as the most attractive in France, Van Gogh was always overlooked. His younger brother Theo had just married and his friend and fellow artist Paul Gaugin was living with him for a time to keep him company. Van Gogh was obsessed with Gaugin who was not only a more successful painter at the time, he was also infinitely more popular with women.

Gaugin was planning to leave the 'Yellow House' in Arles after the pair had quarrelled, perhaps over a woman, and Van Gogh angrily threw a glass at him. As they walked through the town, the argument once more grew heated and Gaugin, an excellent fencer, drew his sword and cut off Van Gogh's left earlobe, possibly in self-defence.

Van Gogh wrapped the bloody ear in a handkerchief and presented it to Rachel, the prostitute who had previously spurned his advances, in a bizarre parody of a love token. The estranged friends made a pact of silence over what had happened and Van Gogh staggered home where he was found the next day.

POODLES AND PANTHERS

It was like feasting with panthers; the danger was half the excitement. Oscar Wilde

From richly rewarded Parisian courtesans parading their equally pampered pooches, to street walkers, bawds, rent boys and transvestites, everything was for sale on city streets and you didn't have to look far to find it. Dangerous liaisons, clandestine meetings, and not-so-secret scandals were to be found in theatres, arcades, public parks, hotels, and behind closed doors everywhere. Bribery and corruption were rife but some, like Wilde, paid a heavy price.

By the eighteenth century, despite the threat of punishment, fines, and the notorious Bridewells in England, prostitution was thriving. In European cities such as Paris it tended to be fairly discreet. High-class courtesans, supported by their aristocratic lovers, kept their literary and artistic salons at fashionable addresses, but ordinary working girls and streetwalkers were to be found only in confined areas.

In London, the sex trade was much more widely spread. Poor girls might pick up customers in the alleys off Fleet Street, or take them back to ramshackle lodgings on Drury Lane. Lawyer and author James Boswell was infamous for his dalliances on Westminster Bridge, St James's Park, or wherever the fancy took him, whilst middle-class mistresses entertained in Marylebone, and the wealthiest were set up in the mansions of Mayfair. The Tea or Pleasure Gardens across the capital gave further opportunity for frivolity and debauchery of every kind. Even Samuel Pepys was shocked at the louche behaviour he witnessed at Vauxhall Gardens. But at the centre of it all, the heart of the harlot's trade was Covent Garden.

COVENT GARDEN

Covent Garden piazza in the seventeenth century

Laid out by Inigo Jones for the Duke of Bedford in the early seventeenth century, the elegant piazza and Palladian Italianate houses were immediately popular. When London's flower, fruit and vegetable markets relocated there after the Fire of London, taverns and coffee houses followed swiftly and soon bath houses or 'bagnios' made a reappearance.

People from all classes and walks of life rubbed shoulders most evenings in establishments such as the neighbouring Shakespeare's Head Tavern and Bedford Head Coffee House. You were as likely to find the actors David Garrick and Sarah Siddons as the literary Samuel Johnson, Henry Fielding and Tobias Smollett, and artists including Joshua Reynolds and William Hogarth. The area was a melting pot for the exchange of ideas, politics and gossip. Businessmen and conmen worked out their deals and along with everything else, sex was very definitely on the menu.

HARRIS'S LIST

Most pimps kept some sort of little black book, a who's who of whores and bawds. In essence, Harris's list was the same, just on a far grander scale. Jack Harris was the head waiter at the Shakespeare's Head Tavern and the self-styled 'Pimp General of All England'. His handwritten notebook held the names and addresses of more than four hundred 'votaries of Venus'. He kept it absolutely up-to-date and amended it regularly. Many of the girls were there only for a season, selling themselves as the only commodity they owned when families fell on hard times or ended up in the Fleet Prison for debtors. They appeared one year, earned enough to stand bail, and the next year they were gone. How they reintegrated into respectable society is less clear; perhaps they simply moved to a different parish.

Harris knew them all. And he recorded their ages, prices,

any special services they offered, descriptions of what they looked like, their character and biographical details, plus the important issue of health. With so much information at his disposal, it's no wonder Harris had a reputation for catering to every customer's taste.

It was Samuel Derrick who thought of publishing the list as a book; he had come across it when making use of Harris's services. Derrick had arrived in London from Dublin in 1751, full of ambition, but his fondness for wine and women had drawn him to Covent Garden and luck had not been on his side. Six years later, he found himself in debt in Bailiff Ferguson's sponging house, with only the prospect of Fleet Prison beckoning.

Derrick had seen how much money Harris had made from his handwritten list and thought he could do better. He must have come to some arrangement to use the notes and name, as Harris had quite a reputation as an influential criminal and bully, and he probably paid a one-off permission fee.

Years of personal experience with Covent Garden ladies meant Derrick could add to Harris's notes, and he also included witty anecdotes and quirky inside jokes that would appeal to readers. Derrick found an eager publisher called H. Ranger who advanced him the money needed to clear his debts and avoid prison. Within months, in 1757, the first edition was printed and for sale at two shillings and sixpence. At first it was sold only through the Shakespeare's Head and nearby brothels. Soon it was more widely available and before long it was selling 8,000 copies a year. *Harris's List* proved so popular that it was updated and reprinted every year for almost half a century.

For twelve years Samuel Derrick was the only editor, although no one knew his identity until his death in 1769, when he left the proceeds of the latest edition to Charlotte Hayes, an old friend and courtesan whom he had loved but could not afford. Others, also largely anonymous, took over the list but it was never quite as sparkling or sharp as under Derrick's editorship.

Jack Harris, seeing the success of 'his' list, had tried to publish his own. Called *Kitty's Attalantis*, it couldn't match Derrick's version, and only ran for one edition.

THE HARLOT'S PROGRESS

In the eighteenth century the prevailing view was that prostitutes were most often innocent girls lured to the city then tricked and corrupted by an immoral madam. Whilst the public were generally tolerant of working prostitutes, they were hostile to those who became bawds. Recruiting girls to brothels was seen as evil and it was thought that bawds used trickery to ensnare, resorting to violence and threats to keep the girls.

Hogarth's *The Harlot's Progress* told just such a tale, with the young ingénue Moll Hackabout arriving from the country at the Bell Inn near Cheapside. In his portrayal, Hogarth was taking a satirical swipe at society's morality and his characters represented real people.

Moll was based on Kate Hackabout, who worked for Mother

Needham, a well-known bawd who ran a brothel in fashionable Park Place, St James's. With aristocratic connections and neighbours including various dukes and earls, Elizabeth Needham considered herself immune from prosecution. But she had a reputation as a cruel and harsh employer.

In the first scene of *The Harlot's Progress*, the watching man is the notorious Colonel Charteris and the man dancing around him is probably his pimp, John Gourlay. In 1730, Charteris was sentenced to death for raping the servant girl Ann Bond. Mother Needham was convicted of procuring Ann Bond for Charteris (and so it was said, not the first time she had found him a victim). She was held in the stocks in April 1731, where she was so violently stoned by the angry mob that she died three days later.

Hogarth charted Moll's rise to mistress and her subsequent fall. By scene four she is in prison, still dressed in her fine silks, but forced to beat hemp. The next plate shows her in cheerless lodgings in Covent Garden, dying from tertiary syphilis. In the final scene, Moll lies in her coffin and the whole sad cycle is beginning again.

THE HIERARCHY OF VICE

There was a strict hierarchy of prostitutes in London. At the top of the scale were the educated girls from good but impoverished families who were kept as mistresses, set up in their own houses by their wealthy admirer or client. They tended to live close to the royal palaces, in St James's, Westminster, Mayfair and Marylebone.

Next came the higher-class brothels of St James's and Soho – long associated with the sex trade, which in the eighteenth century was definitely upmarket. These well-appointed bawdy-houses or seraglios copied French salons in style, with the girls sitting around in a central lounge. They frequently offered theatrical entertainments and catered for all tastes. There was a constant demand for virgins and small vials of pigs' blood, or similar, were used to great effect so that a girl might be a 'virgin' many times over.

Nocturnal Night Revels, which claimed to be a genuine guide to brothels, bagnios and seraglios from the 1720s to the 1770s, describes a list of the services and charges offered at Mrs Charlotte Hayes's high-class establishment in King's Place, St James's. Some of the names are probably satirical nicknames for real people. On Sunday (always the busiest night) 9 January 1769, eight clients are listed along with suggested harlots.

'Alderman Drybones' paid 20 guineas for Nelly Blossom, aged nineteen, who 'has had no one for four days, and is a virgin' (again). 'Baron Harry Flagellum' paid 10 guineas presumably to be flogged by a girl no older than nineteen, either Nell Hardy from Bow Street, Bat Flourish from Berners Street, or Miss Birch from Chapel Street.

'Lord Spasm' paid 5 guineas for strong beautiful Black Moll from Hedge Lane, and 'Colonel Tearall' paid 10 guineas for Mrs Mitchell's servant, a 'modest woman', who had just arrived from the country. 'Dr Frettext' wanted an out-of-hours consultation with a woman with 'white skin and a soft hand'; it is fairly obvious what service he paid 2 guineas for to Polly Nimblewrist from Oxford or Jenny Speedyhand from Mayfair.

'Count Alto' paid 10 guineas for an hour with a woman of fashion, either Mrs Smirk from Dunkirk, or Miss Graceful from Paddington, while 'Lord Pyebald' paid 5 guineas for *titillatione mammarum'* to Mrs Tredrille from Chelsea.

It was not just 'gentlemen' who required attention. 'Lady Loveit' paid the vast sum of 50 guineas to be 'well mounted' by Capt O'Thunder or Sawney Rawbone.

The whore houses and garrets of Covent Garden were a step down from the salons of Soho, and beyond that came the street walkers and the most desperate who frequented the alleyways close to the river.

Another harsh reality was child prostitution. In 1777, Mother Sarah Woods was charged with 'harbouring young girls from eleven to sixteen, for the purpose of sending them nightly to parade the streets'. She was caught after the Night Watch officer picked up a girl of twelve together with the servant accompanying her to make sure she didn't run away. Mother Woods worked the girls as servants all day then sent them out as prostitutes at night.

Boys as well as girls who managed to avoid the sex trade were often forced into other criminal activities including begging, stealing or picking the well-lined pockets of the customers who crowded into Covent Garden.

JILTED

The verb 'to jilt', to reject or cast aside a lover, comes from 'Jilt' the mid-seventeenth-century word for a harlot, which is possibly taken from an older Middle English word for a girl, 'jillet' or 'gill'.

HOOKER

It is claimed that the term 'hooker' dates from the time of the American Civil War, 1862–1867. General Joseph Hooker was said to be so fond of a particular row of bawdy houses on Lafayette Square in Washington, DC, that it came to be known as 'Hooker's Row'.

COFFEE AND CAROUSING

A coffee house in Queen Anne's time (1702–14)

London's first coffee house (or rather, coffee stall) was opened by an eccentric Greek named Pasqua Rosée in 1652. While a servant for a British merchant in Smyrna, Turkey, Rosée developed a taste for the exotic Turkish drink and decided to import it to London. People from all walks of life flocked to his business to meet, drink, think, write, gossip and jest, all fuelled by coffee.

It was the coffee houses that were at the hub of nightlife in Covent Garden. The Bedford Head Coffee House was said to be crowded every night with 'men of parts, politicos, scholars and wits' who happily mixed with the celebrities of the day, the whores, the bawds, the pimps and the frankly criminal, all dressed in their finest for a night on the town.

The diarist William Hickey described Weatherby's Coffee House as one of the more outrageous, calling it 'absolute hell on earth'. This does not seem to have been a deterrent to his frequent visits and he wrote with some glee of the scene one evening when the whole place was in uproar, customers perched on tables and benches for a better view of the two women fighting on the floor: 'Two she-devils, for they scarce had a human appearance, were engaged in a scratching and boxing match, their faces entirely covered with blood, bosoms bare, and clothes nearly torn from their bodies.'

The system of entry to Weatherby's was an interesting one. Girls looking for business had to buy a 'capuchin', or milky coffee, to be allowed to join the throng inside.

MOLL KING'S COFFEE HOUSE

One of the most famous of the Covent Garden coffee houses was run by Tom and Moll King. They started with a stall selling nuts in the market, then opened a wooden shack selling 'penny a dish' coffee. By 1717, this had become a thriving coffee house. It opened in the early hours of the morning for the market traders and became famous for its 'nightly revels' and as the 'rendezvous of young Rakes and their Pretty Misses'. Everyone from young bucks to actresses, poets to players, would meet there.

Tom was described as a 'fallen gentleman' educated at Eton and King's College, Cambridge. Moll was the subject of a pamphlet called *The Life and Character of Moll King, late Mistress of King's Coffee House in Covent Garden* that appeared just after her death in 1747. It suggests not only that Moll 'shar'd her favours' but that she took advantage of drunken revellers 'that she might make her Property of both the Gentlemen and their Misses', making sure to keep a clear head herself. The pamphlet also hints that Moll was something of a loan shark, having 'a great many of the poor Females under her Thumb . . . because she lent them money at a high Interest'.

Although never a brothel, as the meeting place of bawds, pimps and their clients, the coffee house attracted plenty of attention and in 1737 Moll and Tom were charged with running a disorderly house. Released on bail, the charge carried a fine rather than a prison sentence.

By 1739 Tom King had drunk himself to death. If anything, the coffee house acquired an even more outrageous reputation but it was so successful that Moll King ended her days as a respectable property owner with a string of houses on Haverstock Hill in Hampstead. Not bad for a street trader who seems also to have dabbled as a prostitute, thief and money lender.

A PARISIAN BORDELLO

A strange book was published in 1779 called *The English Spy; or Secret Correspondence between Milord the Eye and Milord the Ear* which offers a glimpse inside a Parisian brothel of the day. The author remained anonymous and it is not clear how much was fact and how much fiction. However, it paints a graphic picture of Madame Gourdan's bordello, staffed by fake virgins and with hidden entrances to shield customers' and prostitutes' identities. Peepholes, mail-order dildoes, pampering rooms, soundproof torture chambers and erotic boudoirs to arouse the senses were all features.

AND ALL FOR SIX GUINEAS

Women outside a bagnio in 1787

The bath house, that popular feature of the medieval sex trade, made a comeback from the late seventeenth century. Now usually called a 'bagnio', just like the original ones, with the relaxed dress code, semi-naked clients and mix of men and women, getting clean was rarely the first priority.

Official, above-board services included shaving, washing, sweating and cupping, where heated glasses were placed on the body to draw out toxins or blood, to reduce inflammation and treat a range of common ailments. Unofficially they were the clandestine meeting places for men and women. It was also possible for customers to state their preferences, whereupon suitable women, or men, would arrive promptly by sedan chair.

Bagnios sprang up across the capital wherever there was a suitable water supply and there were several in Covent Garden alone: Haddock's, Lovejoy's, and the Bedford Arms Tavern and Bagnio among the more famous. Casanova on a visit to London in 1763 recorded his visit to the bagnios in his memoirs:

> . . . where a rich man can sup, bathe and sleep with a
> fashionable courtesan, of which species there are many
> in London. It makes a magnificent debauch, and only
> costs six guineas.

The German historian Johann Archenholz also left a detailed account:

> In London there is a certain kind of house, called
> bagnios, which are supposed to be baths; their real
> purpose, however, is to provide persons of both sexes
> with pleasure. These houses are well and often richly

*furnished, and every device for exciting the senses is
either at hand or can be provided. Girls do not live here,
but they are fetched in sedan chairs when required.
None but those who are specially attractive in all ways
are so honoured, and for this reason they often send
their address to a hundred of these bagnios in order
to make themselves known. A girl who is sent for and
does not please receives no gratuity, the chair alone
being paid for . . . All noise and uproar is banned here,
no loud footsteps are heard, every corner is carpeted
and the numerous attendants speak quietly amongst
themselves. Old people and degenerates can here receive
flagellation, for which all establishments are prepared.*

Archenholz also explained why some bawdy houses were
called bagnios:

*In every bagnio is found a formula regarding baths,
but they are seldom needed. These pleasures are very
expensive, but in spite of this many houses of this
kind are full every night. Most of them are quite
close to the theatres, and many taverns are in the
same neighbourhood.*

THE TOAST OF THE TOWN

From the time of the Restoration, engravings showing Charles II's mistresses had proved popular. At first it was only royal courtesans who were depicted, but soon images of other famous harlots and actresses fêted as the 'Toast of the Town' also began appearing. These began as straightforward portraits but before long caricatures and satirical prints were widely circulated.

Kitty Fisher, one of the most famed actress courtesans, was such a popular subject that when she was thrown from her horse while riding in St James's Park in March 1759 the 'merry incident' inspired months of songs, drawings, pamphlets, and even a book. She became so incensed at some of the stories and pictures of her that were being printed that she commissioned the famous artist Sir Joshua Reynolds to paint her portrait so that at least a more appealing and representative image would appear.

This was the start of a new direction for Reynolds. Already famous for his idealized portraits, he painted most of the celebrity figures of his time. Working rapidly, he sometimes saw up to six clients in a day, amongst them many other courtesans and members of the demi-monde.

Kitty Fisher also took out an advert in *The Public Advertiser* to set the record straight:

> *She has been abused in public papers, exposed in print-shops and to wind up the whole, some wretches, mean, ignorant and venal, would impose upon the public, by*

> *daring to pretend to publish her Memoirs. She hopes to*
> *prevent the success of their endeavours, by thus publicly*
> *declaring that nothing of that sort has the slightest*
> *foundation in truth.*

Casanova, on his 1763 visit, wangled himself an introduction. As he was penniless at the time and spoke little English, Kitty is unlikely to have been overimpressed. He described her living in the greatest splendour, with liveried servants, fine dresses and diamonds. The historian Archenholz claimed she knew her merit and 'demanded a hundred guineas for a night' and was never short of admirers.

Another particularly colourful anecdote records Kitty eating a banknote on a slice of bread and butter for breakfast. The size of the note varies between a £20 and £50 bill, but it was said to have been a tip left by the Duke of York that Kitty found so paltry she refused to see him again.

Reynolds painted Kitty many times and his diary shows numerous appointments over the years. He famously depicted her as Cleopatra and he kept an unfinished portrait of her with him all his life.

At some point in either 1765 or 1767, Kitty married John Norris of Hempstead Manor, Benenden in Kent. He was described as a country gentleman but nothing more is known of him. Kitty died shortly after and is buried in the churchyard at Benenden.

A TALE OF TWO WOMEN

Of all the Toasts of the Town, Lavinia Fenton's story was one of the most successful. Born a bastard, Lavinia's mother had been cruelly deceived and abandoned with her small baby girl. Her reputation ruined, she moved to London and soon married Mr Fenton, who kept a coffee house on the Charing Cross Road. Not the ideal place for a vivacious young girl, Lavinia was sent away to boarding school, but at seventeen she became the mistress of a Portuguese nobleman who promised to reward her generously. In the event, his debts caught up with him first and he was thrown into the Fleet prison.

Lavinia resolved to earn enough money to buy her lover's freedom and using her wit, charmed her way into a theatre company. She first appeared on stage in 1726 and then played the part of Cherry Boniface in a new production of Farquhar's *The Beaux' Stratagem*. At this point fate stepped in and John Rich took her on as an actress with a regular wage, appearing at his playhouse in Lincoln's Inn Fields.

When it was discovered that Lavinia could sing well she secured the part of Polly Peachum in John Gay's *The Beggar's Opera*, although she was not yet twenty. The part was to change her life. The play became an overnight success and Lavinia an instant star, the most celebrated Toast of the Town.

By 1728, she had become the mistress of the Duke of Bolton and on the death of his wife in 1751 the Duke married her. It had taken over twenty years, but Lavinia ended her days as the wealthy, titled and eminently respectable Duchess of Bolton.

Sally Salisbury's story did not end well, but was perhaps more typical. Born Sally Shrewsbury in 1692, it was obvious from a young age that Sally would be a beauty. She was clever and witty, but also had a wild streak and a hot temper. She left the milliner to whom she was apprenticed to work as an orange girl at Drury Lane Theatre, and there seems to have fallen into the clutches of the evil Colonel Charteris. She was soon working in Elizabeth Wisebourne's bawdy house in Drury Lane, where she changed her name to Salisbury after being told she looked like the Countess of Salisbury.

Sally was extremely popular at Mother Wisebourne's (sometimes known as Whyburn) and among her lovers were the Prince of Wales (later George II), the Duke of Richmond, and the Duke of St Albans, son of that other famous orange seller Nell Gwyn.

In 1713, she caused a riot at Mother Wisebourne's, attracting the kind of attention the bawd had managed to avoid for years. Sally was drunk and disorderly and sent to Newgate prison, though not for long. Judge Blagney was captivated by her and she was released. At this time one of her admirers, possibly Blagney himself, took a house for her, but this arrangement did not last long and Sally was soon back working for Mother Wisebourne and was there when the ageing bawd died in 1719.

After this, Sally moved to Park Place, St James's, a far more fashionable neighbourhood, but to the brothel of the far stricter Mother Needham. It was there in 1722 that she stabbed her lover,

Lord Finch, in a fit of temper. He whispered, 'I die at pleasure by your hand', as he swooned in her arms but actually recovered.

Sally was arrested and found herself back in Newgate. Lord Finch, a forgiving man and besotted with his fiery mistress, did everything in his power to help, offering legal advice and hampers of food. Sally however, developed a brain fever, probably as a result of syphilis, and she died in 1724 at the age of thirty-two.

MOLLY HOUSES

Alongside the brothels, bagnios and coffee houses, there were also the 'molly houses', as homosexual brothels were usually called.

Punishments for male prostitutes were considerably harsher than for female ones. Women convicted of prostitution could face at worst a prison sentence but more often a fine, depending upon their social class and how well connected their clients were. For men, sodomy was not only illegal but still a capital offence since Henry VIII's Buggery Act of 1533, which remained on the statute books. Although in practice most judges were reluctant to recommend a death penalty, homosexuality carried a long prison sentence and hard labour, and even hints were enough to ruin a man's reputation.

In 1707, a molly house in the City was raided and forty men who frequented the alleys and narrow streets around the Royal Exchange were arrested. Of those, four men killed themselves rather than face scandal: William Grant, a draper, hanged himself in Newgate; Jacob Ecclestone, a merchant, committed suicide in the same prison; and Mr Jermain, a curate of St Dunstan's-in-the-East, and Mr Bearden, profession unknown, both slashed their own throats.

Most information comes from trials, newspapers and anonymous pamphlets. The Old Bailey records suggest there was a sudden toughening of attitudes at the end of the 1720s. Before then, trials were relatively rare and few men were found guilty. There were ten sodomy trials between 1726 and 1728 with most of the accused found guilty and four executed. After this series of sensationalized cases the mood calmed, and in 1729 there were only two trials, both of which ended in not-guilty verdicts.

MOTHER CLAP'S

Raids focused on areas known to be popular with homosexuals, including St Paul's and the Barbican, Moorfields, Cheapside, the south side of St James's Park, Fleet Street and of course, Covent Garden. But the particular area of interest was Saffron Hill in Holborn, and most famous of all, Mother Clap's Molly House on Field Lane, Holborn.

Elizabeth Clap was an ageing bawd whose surname was probably a reference to the pox rather than her real name. When her molly house was raided in 1726, Thomas Newton turned King's evidence to save his own skin. He described the establishment: 'It bore the publick Character of a Place of

Entertainment for Sodomites, and for the better Conveniency of her Customers, she had provided Beds in every Room in her House.' It catered for thirty to forty men most nights but more on a Sunday, which was the most popular night of the week for assignations.

Another witness named as Samuel Stephens seems to have been an undercover investigator. He remembered the patrons 'hugging, kissing and tickling each other' as they sat on one another's laps:

> *I have been there several times, and seen twenty or*
> *thirty of 'em together, making Love, as they call'd it,*
> *in a very indecent Manner. Then they used to go out*
> *by Pairs, into another Room, and at their return, they*
> *would tell what they had been doing together, which*
> *they call'd marrying.*

Mother Clap was herself put on trial. Running the molly house was a far less serious charge than sodomy, and there was no question of a death penalty, but she faced a fine, imprisonment and, most dangerous in terms of personal safety, she would be made to stand in the pillory and face whatever the baying mob chose to throw at her. Injuries sustained could be serious and even lead to death, as in the case of Mother Needham in 1731.

'TWO KISSING GIRLS OF SPITALFIELDS'

Lesbians generally attracted less attention, although a balladeer of 1728 immortalized Jenny and Bess from Spitalfields in east London, saying, 'She kisses all, but Jenny is her dear, She feels her Bubbies, and she bites her ear.'

Sisters Anne and Elanor Redshawe ran what they called 'an extremely secretive discreet House of Intrigue' in Tavistock Street, catering for 'Ladies in the Highest Keeping', and there was also 'Mother Courage' of Suffolk Street. Meanwhile, lesbian relationships were not uncommon between prostitutes, and Cleland's eponymous hero Fanny Hill was first introduced to the pleasures of the flesh by an older woman. There are references in *Harris's List*, for instance Miss Wilson of Green Street, Cavendish Square:

> ... *Her hands and arms, her limbs, indeed, in general,*
> *are more calculated for the milk-carrier, than the soft*
> *delights of love; however, if she finds herself but in*
> *small estimation with our sex, she repays them the*
> *compliment, and frequently declares that a female bed-*
> *fellow can give more real joys than ever she experienced*
> *with the male part of the sex ... Many of the pranks*
> *she has played with her own sex in bed (where she is as*
> *lascivious as a goat) have come to our knowledge ...*

An Italian courtesan called Catherine Vizzani was not so fortunate. She was shot dead in 1755 attempting to elope with a woman whilst dressed as a man.

DON'T FRIGHTEN THE HORSES

The pattern of tacit tolerance, an out-of-sight-out-of-mind attitude, interspersed with the occasional clampdown and high-profile case, continued through the eighteenth and much of the nineteenth centuries.

When the Member of Parliament for Dorset was discovered in the shadows of Westminster Abbey with a soldier named Flower, professors, clergy and aristocratic members of the House were quick to act as character witnesses to his otherwise blameless reputation. When the same MP, William Bankes, was caught again, this time with a guardsman in Green Park, he knew the game was up. He fled abroad in 1841 before he could be brought to trial.

Stories circulated. There were rumours that the charismatic politician George Canning, who was briefly Prime Minister in 1827, had a fondness for effete young men and the colleges of Oxford and Cambridge were said to provide a welcome all-male preserve for some. But such stories were usually quickly forgotten; there were, however, others that captured everyone's attention.

BOYS WILL BE BOYS?

Ernest Boulton, was the son of a city stockbroker and was himself a stockbroker. Frederick Park was the son of a judge and articled to a solicitor. Close friends, they had both, since boyhood, enjoyed dressing up. By their early twenties they had found their way into London's homosexual underworld, where they wore women's clothes and posed as sisters. Ernest, who was the more charismatic and better-looking of the pair, was Stella, and Frederick called himself Fanny.

They were quite brazen in their behaviour, flirting with men at theatres, soliciting in the Burlington Arcade and frequenting private drag balls. They also seem to have been promiscuous. Stella took a lover to Scarborough, where she appeared on stage in a drag act to great acclaim; the press hailed it as a hilarious prank. Both Fanny and Stella revelled in male attention, although Stella was generally held to be the more convincing woman.

Their behaviour did not go unnoticed, and when they were arrested at the packed Strand Theatre on 28 April 1870, police had been tracking them for over a year. The tide of public opinion was turning and becoming more conservative, at least on the surface. This was the Victorian age after all.

When the police raided Boulton's and Park's lodgings in Mayfair and Buckingham Palace Road, they found trunks full of dresses, petticoats, wigs, padding and a copious amount of chloroform, used as a mild aphrodisiac and muscle relaxant at the time.

The pair were carted off to Newgate prison, where they had to undergo a detailed, humiliating examination by six doctors, literally probing for signs of sodomy for two hours. Four warders, two orderlies, and three detectives, along with the duo's solicitor and an official from the Treasury upholding the public interest, were also there.

When Boulton and Park finally stood trial in May 1871, their case was a national sensation. The courtroom was packed and there were daily debates in the newspapers. Among their associates were Lord Arthur Clinton, son of the Duke of Newcastle, and the American consul to Edinburgh, John Safford Fiske.

Letters between Boulton and Lord Arthur were read out in court: 'I am consoling myself in your absence by getting screwed' and 'I have as usual left a few things behind, such as the glycerine, etc, but I cannot find those filthy photos, I do hope they are not lying about your room'.

Lord Arthur died just a few weeks after Boulton's and Park's arrest. At the time there were loud whispers that he had faked his death and fled to Europe. Fiske was taken in for questioning and offered to step down, but was persuaded against doing so, as it was hardly fitting for a diplomat to resign on Newgate prison writing paper.

Surgeons had found no evidence of anal sex, which presented Lord Chief Justice Cockburn with something of a dilemma. Boulton and Park might be self-confessed transvestites but without actual proof, they could not be convicted of sodomy. There was no evidence they had ever tried to rob or blackmail any of their male conquests and Park's landlady had testified clearly that there was no evidence of immorality.

The judge in his summing up condemned the pair's 'frolic' as 'an outrage not only of public morality, but also of decency', but there were no grounds for conviction and Boulton and Parks were pronounced not guilty and released.

One significant side effect of the case was that it drew attention to what had been going on. A senior police officer told a House of Lords committee in 1881: 'There is a considerable amount of sodomy practised in London. It is a fact, and it is an undisputable fact, there are boys and youths soliciting in the streets.' And it was not just the capital. Across the country police were raiding brothels where they found teenage boys as well as girls. The newspapers began warning that Britain was sinking beneath a weight of 'filth, immorality and disease'.

FEASTING WITH PANTHERS

The cause célèbre and case that rocked society and sent newspapers flying off the shelves with details of the latest lurid instalment was the trial of Oscar Wilde. His story and downfall came to represent the decadence of the fin de siècle.

Arriving at Magdalen College Oxford in 1874, Wilde had affected the flamboyant style of dress and conduct that was to be his signature for the rest of his life. He enthusiastically embraced the Aesthetic Movement under the tutelage of the eccentric don Walter Pater and its motto 'Art for Art's sake'. Aesthetes shared a Platonic appreciation of male beauty and homosexual tendencies were not unacceptable. The worst 'punishment' meted out to anyone by the non-aesthetic 'hearties' was debagging and dumping in the college fountain.

Graduating from Oxford, Wilde announced, 'I'll be a poet, a writer, a dramatist. Somehow or other I'll be famous, and if not famous, I'll be notorious.' He was to get his wish.

As expected of him, Wilde was soon married to Constance Lloyd, and they had two sons. In London, his brilliance and charisma drew an admiring entourage, among them Robbie Ross. In 1886, Ross, aged seventeen, had dropped out of Cambridge and knew exactly what his preferences were sexually. He was devoted to Wilde and determined to seduce him.

The relationship with Ross marked a change for Wilde. He seems to have accepted his own sexuality from this point and avoided sex with Constance. His writing career also took off with the publication of *The Picture of Dorian Gray* in 1890, followed by four society comedies, which made him one of the most successful playwrights in late Victorian Britain.

It was at this time that Wilde commented: 'I wanted to eat of the fruit of all the trees in the garden of the world', and he began to have multiple male partners. He also met Lord Alfred Douglas or 'Bosie'. They seem to have become lovers around 1892, but Bosie was careless. He regularly sought out rent boys, many of whom had police records, and more than once found himself being blackmailed by one of his young male lovers. This added to the frisson of danger for Wilde. But rumours began to circulate about the pair.

Wilde's downfall began when Bosie gave one of his old suits to Alfred Wood, one of the renters. In the pockets were passionately explicit letters from Wilde. Wood planned to blackmail them and Wilde paid him off, however one of the letters found its way to Bosie's father, the Marquess of Queensberry, and from that moment on Wilde's fate was sealed.

Queensberry bad-mouthed Wilde and accused him of sodomy. Despite advice from friends, particularly Ross, that he should ignore the accusations, Wilde sued the Marquess for libel, largely encouraged by Bosie. The trial against Queensberry was to bring to light evidence that not only forced Wilde to drop his charges but would lead to his arrest for gross indecency with other men. The 1895 trial ran with increasingly sensational evidence. It is a testament to Wilde that in the middle of it all he was able to write *The Importance of Being Earnest*.

At the end of the trial the judge ruled in Queensberry's favour and the Marquess left the courtroom to cheers of approval. Wilde was not there. With all the evidence going against him he had the opportunity to flee to Europe and avoid a greater scandal. Instead, he famously stayed at the Cadogan Hotel, where he was arrested.

Wilde went on trial at the Old Bailey for gross indecency on 26 April 1895 after spending a long month in prison. Signs of the strain were already beginning to show in his appearance and his usually long hair was cut short to meet prison regulations. It was during the court proceedings that he made his now famous speech:

The 'Love that dare not speak its name' in this century
is such a great affection of an elder for a younger
man as there was between David and Jonathan, such
as Plato made the very basis of his philosophy, and
such as you find in the sonnets of Michelangelo and
Shakespeare. It is the deep, spiritual affection that is as
pure as it is perfect . . .

When Wilde stood to hear the verdict, he was informed that the jury had failed to reach a decision and a third trial was scheduled. On 24 May 1895 the judge condemned Wilde as guilty, commenting that it was the worst case he had ever heard and that he therefore had no choice but to pass 'the severest sentence that the law allows'. Wilde was sent to Reading jail for two years' hard labour.

Upon his release in 1897 he left for exile in France. Afraid of guilt by association, few of his old friends would have anything to do with him. Wilde never really recovered from his time in prison and died in Paris in 1901. Robbie Ross was with him to the last and his ashes were later placed in Wilde's tomb at Père Lachaise cemetery.

DEAR DIARY AND
NOTES TO A FRIEND

Lay long in bed today with my wife, merry and pleasant.
The Diary of Samuel Pepys, 6 July 1662

Samuel Pepys

When it comes to being frankly honest, few people are as candid as they are in their diaries. Thoughts, opinions, desires, secrets, in short all those details that are not usually broadcast to the world may be read in the pages of a diary. Letters home, particularly when written from abroad, can also be surprisingly explicit. Perhaps it is the safe distance, or the loosening of the usual bonds of propriety that comes with travel.

'MIND MAKES THE MAN'

This motto was written in Latin on Samuel Pepys' bookplate at the start of his diary. The first entry dates from 1 January 1660 and Pepys recorded his daily life for almost ten years. From the beginning he juxtaposes his personal life and opinions with national and political events. He gives an unrivalled first-hand account of Restoration life, an insight into the monarch Charles II's character, and describes major events such as the Anglo-Dutch War and the disasters of the Great Plague of 1665 and the Fire of London in 1666. As Robert Latham, the editor of his diaries, remarked:

> *They are written with compassion. As always with*
> *Pepys it is people, not literary effects, that matter.*

Written in shorthand and with some passages in French and other languages, it is from Pepys that we learn the details of the king's mistresses. He was there from the start. He comments on 13 July 1660: 'The King and Dukes there with Madam Palmer (Barbara Villiers, later Lady Castlemaine), a pretty woman that they have a fancy to make her husband a cuckold'.

On the day of the royal wedding when a disconsolate Barbara Villiers hung out her washing, Pepys wrote: 'And in the privy Garden saw the finest smocks and linen petticoats of my Lady Castlemaine. Laced with rich lace at the bottoms that ever I saw; and did me good to look upon them.'

Pepys also saw Nell Gwyn before King Charles did. He always had an eye for the orange girls and he was impressed by Nell's comedic performances on stage. In 1667 he says: '. . . saw pretty Nelly standing at her lodgings door in Drury Lane in her smock-sleeves and bodice, looking upon one – she seemed a mighty pretty creature.'

To a large degree, Pepys lived vicariously through the king's exploits, although he was often shocked by what went on at court. He was also unimpressed by Charles's lack of discretion and the fact that he was more concerned with his mistresses than the affairs of state. As an organized administrator and shrewd businessman, Pepys was more than once frustrated by arriving for a meeting only to find there was no paper because the stationery bill had not been paid.

Pepys is humorously deprecating of his own frequent lack of success and unrequited lusts, and is always disarmingly honest about himself. He frequented London's brothels and kept a mistress called Betty Lane who he would visit bearing wine, prawns and lobster. This did not stop him eyeing others and in particular he harboured amorous feelings towards his servant Mary Mercer. On 18 April 1666, having 'saluted' black Nan again and again, 'which pleases me mightily', he went home to bed, but not before touching Mercer's breasts with great pleasure. He later described them as 'the finest that I ever saw in my life; that is the truth of it'.

Throughout, whatever extra Pepys might have got up to, he was genuinely attached to his wife Elizabeth, who he had married in 1655. He obviously enjoyed her company and missed her when they were apart. It is a mark of his feelings that after her sudden death from typhoid fever in 1669, the ever-diligent Pepys took four weeks away from work. He apologized to fellow politicians and naval captains for his failure to keep up to date with correspondence or to attend board meetings.

It is also from Pepys that we learn of the antics of Sir Charles Sedley, MP, wit and libertine. Sedley was part of the so-called 'Merry Gang' of courtiers that included the Earl of Rochester and Lord Buckhurst. In his diary of 1 July 1663, Pepys records a dinner conversation about an incident that had taken place at Oxford Kate's Cock Inn Tavern on Bow Street when Sedley had appeared on the balcony in broad daylight and there:

> *. . . showed his nakedness, acting all the postures of lust and buggery that could be imagined and abusing of scripture. He then claimed he could make and sell a potion 'as should make all the cunts in town run after him'. As the crowd beneath gathered to watch the spectacle, Sedley 'took a glass of wine and washed his prick in it and then drank it off; and then took another and drank the King's health'.*

Sedley found himself arrested for this escapade and given a stern reprimand: 'The Judges did all of them round give him a most high reproof; My Lord Chief Justice saying: That it was for him, and such wicked wretches as he was, that God's anger and judgments hung over us.' He was also fined 2,000 marks. Banished from court for a few weeks to compose himself at his country house, his career did not suffer. He was later to become Speaker of the Commons.

Sedley was a strong supporter of William of Orange and Mary, opposing the Catholic King James II in the Glorious Revolution of 1688. Upon hearing that the king had seduced his daughter and created her Countess of Dorchester he famously commented: 'As the king has made my daughter a countess, the least I can do, in common gratitude, is to assist in making his Majesty's daughter [Mary] a queen.'

'EVERY JOHNSON NEEDS HIS BOSWELL'

James Boswell was born in Edinburgh in 1740 and was a lawyer and author. He is famous for his biography of Samuel Johnson and for his journals, which he kept meticulously. In contrast to his constant companion, Johnson, Boswell was a bon viveur and enthusiast for London's seamier underside.

On Friday 19 November 1762, it was apparently extremely cold, but this did not dampen Boswell's spirits:

> *When we came upon Highgate Hill and had a view of*
> *London, I was all life and joy . . . I sung all manner of songs,*
> *and began to make one about an amorous meeting with a*
> *pretty girl, the burthen of this was as follows:*
> *She gave me this, I gave her that;*
> *And tell me, had she not tit for tat?*

His *London Journal* of 1762–3 noted that the city was full of 'free-hearted ladies of all kinds' and that a 'splendid madam' cost fifty guineas a night. At the other end of the scale were the street walkers, 'a civil nymph with white-thread stockings who tramps along the Strand' will 'resign her engaging person to your honour for a pint of wine and a shilling'. At the time a shilling was the weekly rent for a basement room or garret in one of the poorer parts of London. On 25 March 1763 Boswell records:

> *As I was coming home this night, I felt carnal inclinations raging through my frame. I determined to gratify them. I went to St James Park and picked up a whore. For the first time did I engage in armour [a condom] which I found but a dull satisfaction. She who submitted to my lusty embraces was a young Shropshire girl, only 17, very well-looked, her name Elizabeth Parker. Poor being, she has a sad time of it!*

A few days later on 31 March he was less happily satisfied:

> *At night I strolled into the park and took the first whore I met, whom I, without many words, copulated with free from danger, being safely sheathed. She was ugly and lean and her breath smelt of spirits. I never asked her name. When it was done, she slunk off. I had a low opinion of this gross practice and resolved to do it no more.*

He obviously got over his shame and on 17 May he wrote:

> *So I sallied to the streets, and just at the bottom of our own, I*
> *picked up a fresh, agreeable young girl called Alice Gibbs. We*
> *went down a lane to a snug place, and I took out my armour,*
> *but she begged that I might not put it on, as the sport was*
> *much pleasanter without it, and as she was quite safe. I was*
> *so rash as to trust her, and had a very agreeable congress.*

By the next day Boswell was worrying about his lack of
protection the night before:

> *Much concern was I in from the apprehension of being again*
> *reduced to misery, and in so silly a way too. My benevolence*
> *indeed suggested to me to put confidence in the poor girl; but*
> *then said cool reason, 'What abandoned, deceitful wretches*
> *are these girls, and even supposing her honest, how could she*
> *know with any certainty that she was well?'*

Condoms were hardly a new invention. The Romans had
made them out of leather and the Egyptians from linen, but the
so-called Colonel Condom developed a new way of making them
from cleaned animal gut in 1665. The condoms had to be soaked in
water to make them supple and then after use they could be washed
ready to use again. A ribbon tied them on. They became popular
as a protection against venereal disease rather than to prevent
pregnancy. They were rarely carried by prostitutes walking the
streets and instead were supplied by prepared punters.

Boswell quickly put aside his fears of infection and on the

evening of 19 May had a high old time with two pretty girls in the Shakespeare's Head in Covent Garden:

> *I sallied forth to the Piazzas in a rich flow of animal spirits and burning with fierce desire . . . and then I solaced my existence with them, one after the other, according to their seniority. I was quite raised as the phrase is.*

He went home in a 'glow of spirits'. As this took place in a room in a tavern, Boswell classified it as a 'high debauch' rather than a 'low debauch' on the streets. High or low, unfortunately he had caught gonorrhoea during his revels.

On another occasion Boswell returned to an old haunt, writing in his journal for 25 March 1768:

> *I then went to Covent Garden and in one of the courts called for a young lady whom I had seen when formerly in London. I did not find her, but I found Kitty Brookes, as pretty a lively lass as youth need see. The oil was called and I played my part well. I never saw a girl more expert at it. I gave her only four shillings, to try her generosity. She never made the least sign of discontent, but was quite gay and obliging.*

In many ways Boswell reflects the morality of the times. He often expresses disgust at the whores' behaviour which is probably more a reflection of his feelings towards himself. He sometimes appears shocked at his own weakness and the willingness with which he succumbs to debauchery. He has a taste for rough public sex which at times excites him and at others appals him, but he never seems to wonder at the scale of the sex industry or the number of girls driven to earn their living on the streets. Boswell condemns the idea of corrupting an innocent girl but eases his conscience with the thought: 'When the woman is already abandoned, the crime must be alleviated'.

Boswell was a member of The Club founded by Sir Joshua Reynolds and Samuel Johnson for dining, drinking, literary discussion and debate. Other members included David Garrick, Edmund Burke and Oliver Goldsmith. From 1764 meetings were held at the Turk's Head Tavern on Gerrard Steet in Soho, which made a convenient starting or stopping-off point for meeting the girls who lived and worked in the surrounding area.

Johnson held very different views from his biographer and companion. One night in July 1763 when the pair were walking along the Strand, a girl approached them. Johnson gently refused her and then talked at length to Boswell about the wretched lives such women lived concluding that 'much more misery than happiness, upon the whole, is produced by illicit commerce between the sexes'.

And Johnson practised what he preached. Boswell describes in his *Life of Johnson* how his friend helped a Scottish woman called Polly Carmichael:

> *Coming home late one night, he found a poor woman lying*
> *in the street, so much exhausted that she could not walk; he*

took her upon his back, and carried her to his house, where
he discovered that she was one of those wretched females who
had fallen into the lowest state of vice, poverty and disease.
Instead of harshly upbraiding her he had her taken care of
with all tenderness for a long time, at considerable expense,
till she was restored to health, and endeavoured to put her
into a virtuous way of living.

Things did not completely work out. Johnson later confessed to his friend Mrs Hester Thrale that 'we could spare her well from us. Poll is a stupid slut.' In 1777, Johnson had seven extra people living with him. In her memoirs, Mrs Thrale described his house in Bolt Court as, 'overrun with all sorts of strange creatures, whom he admits for mere charity'.

According to Boswell, after the death of his wife Tetty in 1752, Johnson chose to remain celibate. Johnson rebuffed 'women of the town', and said he wasn't interested in their carnal delights. He told David Garrick, the actor (who told Boswell), that he would not go backstage at the theatre any more because 'the white bubbies and silk stockings of your Actresses excite my genitals'.

CASANOVA

His name is synonymous with lotharios, although that is probably more to do with his twelve volumes of memoirs in which he details each and every conquest. Born in Venice in 1725, he was obviously multitalented or well connected. He was made an abbot at the age of fifteen, a Doctor of Law at sixteen, after which he turned his back on a career in the Church and became amongst other things a poet, historian, businessman, ambassador, violinist, duellist and magician.

It was in the house of the Abbé Gozzi that he first learned to play the violin. It was also there that he had his first sexual experience with Gozzi's younger sister Bettina. He was eleven:

> *The girl pleased me at once, though I had no*
> *idea why. It was she who little by little kindled*
> *in my heart the first sparks of a feeling which*
> *later became my ruling passion.*

IN PRAISE OF OLDER WOMEN

Famously one of the Founding Fathers of the United States, Benjamin Franklin was a leading author, political theorist, statesman, scientist, inventor, musician and noted polymath. Born in 1706, in Milk Street, Boston, Massachusetts, the son of a chandler and candle maker, Franklin was proud of his humble beginnings.

He gained international fame for his scientific experiments with electricity and played a major role in the establishment of the University of Pennsylvania. He was a diplomat, appointed American minister to Paris, and was the British postmaster for the colonies. Governor of Pennsylvania from 1785 to 1788, he became a prominent abolitionist, freeing his own slaves.

Of far less political importance, but offering a colourful glimpse into his character, is a letter of advice he wrote to a young acquaintance on 25 June 1745 from Philadelphia:

> *I know of no medicine fit to diminish the violent natural inclinations you mention, and if I did, I think I should not communicate it to you. Marriage is the proper remedy. It is the most natural state of man, and therefore the state in which you are most likely to find solid happiness . . .*

> *But if you will not take this counsel and persist in thinking a commerce with the sex inevitable, then I*

repeat my former advice, that in all your amours you
should prefer older women to young ones.

You will call this a paradox and demand my reasons.
They are these:

1. Because they have more knowledge of the world and
their minds are better stored with observations, their
conversation is more improving and more lastingly
agreeable
2. Because when women cease to be handsome they study
to be good
3. Because there is no hazard of children
4. Because through more experience they are more prudent
and discreet
5. Because in every animal that walks upright the deficiency
of the fluids that fills the muscles appears first in the
highest part. The face first grows lank and withered.
And as in the dark all cats are grey, the pleasure of
corporal enjoyment with an old woman is at least equal,
and frequently superior; every knack being, by practice,
capable of improvement
6. Because the sin is less. The debauching a virgin may be
her ruin, and make her unhappy for life
7. Because the compunction is less
8th and lastly. They are so grateful!

Franklin spoke from some experience. He had a common-law marriage to Deborah Read, his childhood sweetheart. She had been persuaded to marry John Rogers, who had fled with her dowry and was never traced. As his fate was unknown, Deborah was not allowed to remarry because of strict bigamy laws. Franklin also had an illegitimate son, William, who the couple raised. Franklin never revealed William's mother's name.

OF LOVE AND WAR

Napoleon enjoyed a meteoric rise to power. A supreme general and military tactician, as he marched across Europe, countries crumpled in his path. Ruthlessly ambitious and driven, he was as passionate in his private life.

He met Josephine Beauharnais in 1795, shortly after he had been made Major General, Commandant of the army of the interior. She, like him, was something of an outsider, having been born and brought up in the West Indies. She was also six years his senior, a widow with two children.

Nevertheless, it was love at first sight and they were lovers within weeks, married in months. When the senate were persuaded to make First Consul Bonaparte emperor in 1804, he crowned Josephine his empress. Shortly after their marriage, Napoleon left to conquer Italy and so wrote the first of many love letters. The tone of his missives to Josephine makes it rather less surprising that the manuscript for a romantic novella was discovered amongst his papers. Despite the passion and obvious love between them, both Napoleon and Josephine took other lovers, leading to jealous outbursts.

One of the most famous lines from the manuscript is: 'Will return to Paris tomorrow evening. Don't wash.' But there are so many more:

> *I have not passed a day without loving you; I have not passed a night without holding you in my arms; I have not drunk a cup of tea without cursing the glory and ambition which keeps me so far from the soul of my life.*

> *I demand neither eternal love nor fidelity, but only truth, honesty without limits.*

> *A thousand kisses to your neck, your breasts and lower down, much lower, that little black forest I love so well.*

> *A thousand kisses on your eyes, on your tongue, on your c——. Adorable wife, what is your influence?*

> *I am going to sleep, my little Josephine, my heart full of your adorable image, and sick of spending so long apart from you. But I hope that in a few days, I will be happier, and that I can give you a leisurely proof of the ardent love which you have inspired in me.*

To live in a Josephine is to live in Paradise.

I don't love you, not at all; on the contrary I detest you.
You're a naughty, gawky, foolish slut.

That was the first line. It has to be said he finished the same
letter with:

I hope before long to crush you in my arms and cover you with
a million kisses burning as though beneath the equator.

In April 1796, Napoleon begs Josephine to come to him
in Milan:

'I shall be alone and far, far away. But you are coming, aren't
you? You are going to be here beside me, in my arms, on my
breast, on my mouth? Take wing and come, come . . .

Your tears rob me of reason and inflame my blood.
Believe me it is not in my power to have a single thought
which is not of thee, or a wish I could not reveal to thee.

You no longer write to me. You no longer think of your good
friend, cruel woman! Don't you realise that without you,
without your heart, without your love, your husband has
neither happiness nor life. Good God! How happy I would be
if I could watch you get dressed, your little shoulders, your
little white breasts . . .

*I write you, my beloved one, very often, and you write
very little. You are wicked and naughty, very naughty,
as much as you are fickle.*

*How happy I would be if I could assist you at your
undressing, the little firm white breast, the adorable
face, the hair tied up in a scarf à la créole.*

*Adieu, adorable Josephine; one of these nights your
door will open with a great noise; as a jealous person,
and you will find me in your arms.*

In a letter to his brother, Napoleon wrote of fading love for his empress. It was intercepted by the British and published in all the newspapers to widespread mockery:

*The veil is torn . . . It is sad when one and the same heart
is torn by such conflicting feelings for one person. I need to
be alone. I am tired of grandeur; all my feelings have dried
up. I no longer care about my glory. At twenty-nine I have
exhausted everything.*

MY HEART'S BELOVED

As the co-author of the *Communist Manifesto*, Karl Marx's words sparked revolutions. Even the famous German philosopher had a gentler side. In a letter to his wife Jenny on 21 June 1856, he addresses her as 'My heart's beloved' and goes on to declare: 'I have your photograph vividly before me, and I carry you on my hands, and I kiss you from head to foot, and I fall on my knees before you, and I groan: "Madam, I love you."' So much passion after thirteen years of marriage.

THE PLEASURES OF THE BATHS

Lady Mary Wortley Montagu was not on a Grand Tour. As the wife of the British Ambassador to Turkey, she accompanied him to Istanbul in 1717 and wrote a number of letters enthusiastically describing life in the orient. She was particularly taken with the baths where women would meet:

> *The first sofas were covered with cushions and rich carpets,*
> *on which sat the ladies; and on the second, their slaves behind*
> *them, but without any distinction of rank by their dress, all*
> *being in the state of nature, that is, in plain English, stark*
> *naked, without any beauty or defect concealed . . . I was here*
> *convinced of the truth of a reflection I have often made, that*
> *if it was the fashion to go naked, the face would be hardly*

observed. I perceived that the ladies of the most delicate skins
and finest shapes had the greatest share of my admiration,
though their faces were sometimes less beautiful than those of
their companions.

Women would not only sit chatting, drinking coffee or sherbet, but music and plays would be performed and there were often shops and restaurants. Lady Mary was also fascinated to watch a bridal shower take place there, observing that married women were completely depilated and hairless, which marked them out from the unmarried virgins who still had pubic hair. She noted the complete lack of inhibitions shown in the baths.

Once back in England and living quietly in Twickenham, she became the subject of much speculation that she had herself indulged in the pleasures of the harem.

A FRENCHMAN IN EGYPT

Gustave Flaubert is a renowned French author, known for his attention to detail and vivid character portrayals. Alongside his novels he is also remembered for his correspondence, and he wrote frequent letters to his friends, including George Sand. Always a keen traveller, between 1849 and 1850 Flaubert journeyed extensively with his friend Maxime Du Camp, a journalist, through the Middle East, Greece and Egypt.

In his letters home he is brutally honest about himself,

particularly his sexual exploits. He seems to have considered it almost a duty to experience everything available and wrote explicitly. In his journal, Flaubert explains his interest in prostitutes:

> *It may be a perverted taste, but I love prostitution, and for itself, quite apart from its carnal aspects. My heart begins to pound every time I see one of those women in low-cut dresses walking under the lamplight in the rain, just as monks in their corded robes have always excited some deep ascetic corner of my soul. The idea of prostitution is a meeting place of so many elements – lust, bitterness, complete absence of human contact, muscular frenzy, the clink of gold – that to peer into it deeply makes one reel. One learns so many things in a brothel and feels such sadness and dreams so longingly of love!*

Louis Bouilhet was a poet and dramatist who had been at school with Flaubert and was a lifelong friend. Flaubert wrote to him from Cairo on 15 January 1850, where the baths also featured:

> *Here it is quite accepted. One admits one's sodomy, and it is spoken of at table in the hotel. Sometimes you do a bit of denying, and then everybody teases you and you end up confessing. Travelling as we are for educational purposes, and charged with a mission by the government, we have considered our duty to indulge in this form of ejaculation. So far the occasion has not presented itself. We continue to seek*

> *it, however. It's at the baths that such things take place. You*
> *reserve the bath for yourself (five francs including masseurs,*
> *pipe, coffee, sheet and towel) and you skewer your lad in one*
> *of the rooms.*

Just to complete his sensual journey, Flaubert later described how he pursued one of the most famous dancing girls in Egypt and how flattering it would be if 'you were sure that you left a memory behind, that she would think of you more than of the others who have been there, that you would remain in her heart'.

Upon his return in 1850, Flaubert began work on his masterpiece *Madame Bovary*, which took him five years to complete. The novel was initially serialized in the *Revue de Paris* and the government brought a charge of immorality against both Flaubert and the publisher. At the hearing, they were acquitted and when *Madame Bovary* appeared as a book it was to great acclaim. Flaubert had contracted syphilis on his travels and died in 1880 at the age of fifty-eight.

THE PERFUMED GARDEN

Sir Richard Francis Burton was a scholar, explorer and orientalist. Fascinated by Islam, he was the first European to enter the forbidden city of Mecca and the East African citadel of Harer, disguised in Arab dress.

Travels as a child set the pattern for his life and he showed a talent for language at an early age. He spoke twenty-five, and with dialects the total was brought to almost forty. He published forty-three volumes on his explorations and almost thirty volumes of translations. He was also one of the first real sexologists, collecting facts about sexual customs and techniques wherever he travelled, even recording measurements of penises in different parts of the world.

His interest in sexual behaviour perhaps stemmed from his army days in India. Sir Charles Napier, commander of the British forces in the Sindh, sent Captain Burton, a respected intelligence officer, in disguise to bring back detailed reports from the local bazaar. Then, in 1845, Burton was again sent undercover to investigate the homosexual brothels in Karachi which British soldiers were said to frequent. Burton's explicit report resulted in their destruction but it was so detailed that it led to rumours that he had himself been a customer. These rumours were to follow Burton for the rest of his life, although he may not have troubled himself overly to suppress them. As the French novelist Ouida commented, Burton had a 'Byronic love of shocking people, of telling tales against himself that had no foundation in fact'.

In 1885, he published his celebrated unexpurgated translation of *The Arabian Nights*, or *The Book of the Thousand Nights and One Night*. In ten volumes initially, another six were added later. The stories were invariably sexual in content and were regarded as pornography at the time. The last volume was one of the first English-language texts to tackle the practice of pederasty which Burton argued was prevalent in a region of the southern latitudes that Burton labelled the 'Sotadic zone', after the Classical Greek homo-erotic poet Sotades.

The Obscene Publications Act of 1857 would have made it impossible to publish *The Arabian Nights* without prosecution and a prison sentence, brought by the Society for the Suppression of Vice. A way around the problem was to circulate books privately amongst the members of a society. And so Burton and Forster Fitzgerald Arbuthnot formed the Kama Shastra Society to print and publish otherwise banned books. The Arabian Nights was printed by the Society in a subscribers-only limited edition of a thousand, appropriately enough, with a guarantee there would not be a larger printing of the book in this form.

Burton is also credited with translating the *Kama Sutra* into English. It was written in ancient Sanskrit, which he could not understand, and so he collaborated with Arbuthnot and other Indian scholars. He translated *The Perfumed Garden* from a French edition of the erotic guide and was working on a new edition called *The Scented Garden* when he died in 1890. His widow Isabel burned the manuscript along with journals and other papers, always maintaining this was to protect her husband's reputation.

A WOMAN'S PLACE

The great question that has never been answered, and
which I have not yet been able to answer, despite my
thirty years of research into the feminine soul, is 'What
does a woman want?' Sigmund Freud

By the nineteenth century, the prevailing, largely male view was that ideal women should be charming, submissive and chaste, although it was thought this was at odds with their nature, which was to be emotional, volatile and irrational. The philosopher and early feminist writer Mary Wollstonecraft argued that male educators ruined women by trying to turn them into decorative mistresses rather than letting them be rational human beings, forcing them to conform to the 'opinion that they were created rather to feel than reason'. This created all sorts of problems and a real division between the surface veneer of almost sexless propriety and what was really going on.

The bagnios and brothels remained an accepted feature of life, there was a growing industry around the production of erotic literature and no shortage of customers, and the street walkers and rent boys continued to ply their trade.

FEMALE HYSTERICS

While men failed to understand the female mind, they also failed to understand the workings of the female body and almost seem to have feared it. This is particularly obvious in the widely accepted treatment for the growing problem of 'female hysteria'.

Surely vibrators are a modern invention, openly discussed only after Samantha introduced the rabbit in *Sex and the City*? In fact, vibrators were one of the first appliances to be electrified in the late nineteenth century, not long after the sewing machine but well ahead of the vacuum cleaner. It seems the Victorians had their priorities right. The earliest electromechanical vibrator was developed in 1873 in France (where else?) and initially tried out in an asylum to treat instances of 'female hysteria' amongst inmates.

Shortness of breath, faintness, insomnia, nervousness, loss of appetite for food or sex, headaches, emotional instability and a 'tendency to cause trouble', melancholy, aggression, depression, abdominal heaviness, muscle pains and mood swings were all, not entirely surprisingly, linked to the reproductive cycle. But in the nineteenth century, doctors took them extremely seriously as symptoms of a condition labelled 'female hysteria'. And their preferred treatment? Vaginal massage by the doctor until the woman reached 'hysterical paroxysm' or orgasm.

Since virtually any ailment could fit the diagnosis of female hysteria (one doctor drew up a seventy-five-page catalogue listing the many and varied possible symptoms) and at a time when respectable women were not supposed to experience desire or enjoy sex, it is hardly any wonder that thousands of women hurried to their doctors for urgent alleviation of the problem. By the middle of the nineteenth century, at the height of Victorian morality, it was claimed that up to a quarter of all women were suffering from the condition.

Hysteria was very profitable for doctors to treat, as it was not life-threatening but required repeated, frequent attention. For this reason, doctors were reluctant to pass patients on to midwives or nurses, but they found the treatment time-consuming and fairly tedious, and unsurprisingly often found it hard to bring about hysterical paroxysm. It should be noted that all doctors at this time were male.

The chaise longue and fainting couch became popular to make women more comfortable during the hours it sometimes took to achieve paroxysm. There were even specially designated private fainting rooms and vaginal massage was accepted as a routine medical procedure. To help the overworked doctors, who often quite literally had more patients than they could handle, water sprays and mechanical devices originally intended for sore muscles were developed. At first these vibrators were only for use by doctors, but the spread of electricity to homes led to a growing consumer market for women keen to help themselves.

Adverts for vibrators were common from the 1870s until the 1930s, when a greater general awareness of female sexuality meant they were largely dropped from mainstream advertising as it was no longer possible to focus on their use for muscle massage and ignore what women might really be using them for.

An early portable vibrator

Female hysteria was not a nineteenth-century invention and has a long history. The word itself comes from *hysterikos*, the Greek idea of the womb seeking its proper place and wandering towards the chest and lungs – hence its association with breathlessness. Hippocrates first coined the term and saw sexual dissatisfaction as the main cause, and sex and marriage as the best cures, although he also recommended sneezing.

Some five centuries later, around AD 150, the renowned Roman doctor and philosopher Galen also blamed hysteria on the uterus but did not think it moved around the body. Instead, he believed a lack of sex caused an accumulation of female 'sperm', which produced toxic vapours. His solution was more sex, and for unmarried women pelvic manipulation by a midwife to the point of orgasm. This idea of the vapours continued for centuries, with society women and Victorian grandes dames not infrequently overcome by a fit of 'the vapours', although by then doctors realized no real vapours were involved.

FOR MEN ONLY

And just in case men should feel left out, the nineteenth century also saw numerous adverts for electrical 'cock shocking' belts and beds, promising to cure embarrassing impotence and generate impressive, electrified erections.

One advert for Dr Sanden's Electric Belt and Suspensory from the Sanden Electric Company in Portland, Oregon, demanded: 'Men: Why are you weak?' It went on to claim that its belt was a cure-all for men who were 'debilitated and suffering from nervous debility, seminal weakness, impotency, lost manhood, rheumatism, lame back, kidney troubles, nervousness, sleeplessness, poor memory and general ill health'.

A PORTRAIT OF A MARRIAGE

Few stories reflect the dual standards of society or expose Victorian hypocrisy quite as clearly as that of Arthur Munby and Hannah Cullwick, with its strange contrast of sexual obsession and restraint.

> Took the matting out and moved the fender. Swept the cinders
> up and then undressed me and put on an apron over my head
> and back where I couldn't reach to wash and an old pair of
> boots on as the grate was warm. There's a good space behind
> the grate and I got on a stool and up the chimney out o'sight.

*The soot was thick all round and soft and warm and I lay
in it and fetched a shower or two down wi'my arms and it
trickled over me like a bath. I stopped in the chimney and
thought about Massa and how he'd enjoy seen [sic] me when
I got down. It seemed quite cold out o' the chimney and I got
into the water and washed me. It took me a good while to get
clean and the water I made thick and black.*

The chimney sweep is Hannah Cullwick, a maid of all work at the home of Mr and Mrs Caulfield of Clone House, St Leonard's-on-Sea, Sussex. Hannah wrote this description on 26 April 1865 and sent it to her beloved 'Massa', Arthur Munby, a middle-class civil servant, at the time convalescing after a riding accident.

'Massa' was Hannah's private name for Arthur, a rather uneasy term combining her native Shropshire dialect with overtones of slavery. It reflected their own particular master–slave relationship and Hannah's pleasure at blackening her skin with soot. For much of her life she also wore a leather strap around her right wrist and a locking chain around her neck to which Munby had the key. She was, of course, careful to hide any evidence of this beneath her avowedly sensible dress.

Arthur Munby left boxes filled with diaries and notes, but amongst them he had written virtually nothing about his professional life. His real life's work took place outside office hours. He had a fascination and fetish for big, strong women, particularly working-class women, and more specifically those who did hard, physical, dirty work. When he left his office he would walk for miles, looking at women, following them and talking to them, asking them about the details of their lives. He would sketch them and make notes. He also collected hundreds of photographs of female mine workers, kitchen maids, acrobats, charwomen, milkmaids and fisher wives. By his own account Arthur had little interest in conventional sex and always denied his hobby was anything other than innocent.

One of Arthur's most exciting finds had been a 'tall, hulking wench of eighteen rolling along like a sailor'. When asked her occupation she replied, 'Sir, I scrapes trotters.' This so enthralled him that he accompanied her back to her works at a horn, bone and plasterer's merchants in Bermondsey, where he met another 'trotter-scraper' who was 'splashed all over with lime, and with yellow dirt of an unknown kind'.

In 1854, Hannah was twenty-one and working for Lady Louisa Cotes, who took her to London. Arthur met her on one of his usual walks. He was immediately struck by her height and size – she was over 5 feet 7 inches tall and strongly built. She saw him as the perfect gentleman. The two were kindred spirits and recognized a need in one another.

Their meeting came not long after Hannah had visited the theatre for the first time in her life. She had watched a musical called *The Death of Sardanapalus* based on a play by Lord Byron. It told the story of an ancient king who loved Myrrha, a slave girl who loved him in return but held her own democratic and republican beliefs. The fictional relationship seems to have had a profound effect upon her.

In the summer of 1854, they met as often as Hannah's work duties would allow. She wrote of their first kiss: 'Aye that's why I kissed you first when yo' axed me. It was to see what your mouth was like . . . I knowed you was good by the feel of your mouth. An' I couldna love no man if I didna like his mouth.'

To stay close to Arthur, Hannah began to work in various middle-class households in London. Their relationship broke every rule of social acceptability and had to remain secret. Whilst it was accepted that masters enjoyed sexual favours from their servants, love was quite a different matter and would have offended everyone, including both their families.

Arthur worked at the Ecclesiastical Commissioners' Office and Hannah described visiting him there in 1865. She had to wait around until she judged it was safe to knock at his door and there was no one around to witness her arrival.

> We had a long kiss . . . I licked his boots once of my
> own accord and took my top frock off [she was wearing
> a smart dress over her working clothes] and wrapped
> it up and hid it and my bonnet and the other things
> away. Then Massa looked at my hands and came and
> put 'em alongside his. Mine was brown and looked
> hardworking by his and after that Massa told me to lift
> him up and I did it quite easy and I carried him round
> the room. And then I had to hide myself while the
> servant brought in Massa's beef tea.

Hannah had attended her local charity school between the ages of five and eight and it must be assumed she was a bright pupil. Under Arthur's direction she began to educate herself, managing to attend lectures on literature, biology and French conversation while doing her never-ending chores. *David Copperfield* and anything by Charles Dickens were amongst her favourites. Part of the pact she and Arthur had made was that she would write him detailed descriptions of her daily work with especial attention to the filthy state she was in after her back-breaking jobs were done. The dirtier the task the better for both of them. Arthur was also fascinated by regional accents and would have been attracted to her Shropshire dialect; Hannah added to his knowledge of it in her writing. Altogether Hannah wrote seventeen volumes of diaries plus hundreds of letters. Over the years her style developed confidence and her writing is clear and vivid.

Arthur was obsessed by Hannah's dirty hands and on one occasion she blacked her hand with oil and lead polish to send him a print of it as a Valentine. Hannah was obsessed with licking Arthur's boots. She even dreamed about it:

> *I dreamt as I saw a lady stoop on her knees and lick her husband's boots cause he was going away for a while and so I thought surely if she does such a thing for love I needn't think it too much in licking Massa's boots. I shall do it the more. I thought of when I went to him as I used to of a Sunday and knelt down and licked his boots so many times and so joyfully that Massa wondered what it meant.*

The dirtier the boots the more Hannah liked it. Horse shit was a particular favourite and she claimed she could tell where Massa had been from the taste of his boots.

Hannah Cullwick dressed as a chimney sweep in 1862

On her thirty-first birthday, ten years after they first met, Arthur took Hannah to a photographer. In preparation, Hannah did all her muckiest jobs to make herself as dirty as possible. Dressed in her working clothes, wearing her carpet apron, she called at a public house on her way to the photographer's studio. Blending in with the pub's clientele, she drank a half pint of beer from a pewter tankard that a workman had just drunk from. In the photograph, Hannah looks confidently at the camera lens. Her sleeves are rolled up to show her muscular biceps and the wrist strap. Appropriately, she is pretending to clean boots. Apparently, Arthur and Hannah were disappointed with the results, as she did not look anywhere near dirty enough.

An 1862 photograph of Hannah dressed as a chimney sweep, her skin dark with soot, was more successful. She wrote in her diary: 'Just what I wanted. The rougher-looking, the better.'

Hannah would stay up late writing her diaries and letters, all the while taking care that no one found out for whom she was writing them. Afterwards, she would make her way up to the servants' bedroom in the attic to the bed she shared with another housemaid. After six hours' sleep, another day and another round of chores would begin again, every detail to be recounted in her next letter to Arthur, their favourite theme, her dirtiness. Meeting at his lodgings in Fig Tree Court, Inner Temple, Hannah would re-enact her chores, wearing her work clothes:

> *After we'd petted a bit, Massa asked me if I should like*
> *my face blacked and I said yes, so I got the black lead*
> *and oil out and I knelt twixt his knees and he brushed*
> *my face all over with it until I was a negress like I*
> *was the first time in the little room where I lodged and*
> *Massa came to see me.*

When the pair were together, Hannah would often carry Arthur around and sit him on her lap. Despite the signs of subservience, Hannah remained fiercely independent and in many ways it was she that dictated the terms of their relationship. Throughout her life she worked at several different levels and seems to have preferred the more menial mucky jobs. She had no desire to be passed off as a lady and it took Arthur quite some time to persuade her to marry him. It was not that she did not love him, she explained, but she thought their love was special and unlike that of other people; marriage was irrelevant.

In the event, they were married in secret in 1873. Hannah's family knew but Arthur's were not informed. She moved into Fig Tree Court as his housekeeper to preserve the veneer of public respectability and hide the truth about their relationship. Hannah kept her own surname and insisted that Arthur pay her a wage. It was only during trips abroad that she would reluctantly dress as a lady and play the role of wife. During the summer she would return to Shropshire for working holidays with relatives.

In 1877, Hannah seems to have suffered some sort of breakdown and went to stay with family. When she recovered she went back to domestic service working in Shropshire. After a break, Arthur visited her there regularly until her death on 9 July 1909 at the age of seventy-six. She had spent her last years in a rented cottage near her brother in Shifnal, Shropshire. Her tombstone there in St Andrew's churchyard is inscribed with: 'She was for thirty-six years of pure and unbroken love the wedded wife of Arthur Munby of Clifton Holme in the Wapentake of Bulmer.'

Arthur died the following January aged eighty-one. *Relicta*, his final collection of poems, published in October 1909, was dedicated 'to the gracious and beloved memory of HER whose hand copied out and whose lifelong affection suggested all that is best in this book'. He had at long last confessed his marriage to

Hannah to his brother not long before his death.

In his will, Arthur bequeathed his books and two deed boxes of all his diaries, notes and photographs to the British Museum, who were unable to accept them. Instead they were kept at Trinity College Cambridge with Arthur's instructions that they were not to be opened until 1950, seventy-seven years after his marriage to Hannah. On the opening of the boxes, Hannah's great-niece asked if she could be present. She was told it was a private matter, for family only.

And so the stories continue as they began. In the early years of the twentieth century, Oscar Wilde died in exile in Robbie Ross's arms, memories of his trial and the shock of its revelations still fresh in the public mind; Arthur Munby and Hannah Cullwick enjoyed their own very particular version of a marriage; while Edward VII attracted gossip and speculation over his female friends.

The players and details may change slightly, the freedom to discuss and sexual liberty differ widely across the world, but there is nothing new or modern about today's obsession with sex and secrets. Television and the internet may offer anyone and everyone their fifteen minutes of fame; the passions and obsessions that drive human nature, however, remain the same.

Sexual desire is one of the most basic instincts – that, and an interest in exactly what other people may or may not be getting up to.

*Does it really matter what these affectionate people do
– so long as they don't do it in the streets and frighten
the horses?*
Mrs Patrick Campbell

BIBLIOGRAPHY

Arnold, Catherine, *City of Sin*, Simon & Schuster, 2010.

Aronson, Theo, *The King in Love: Edward VIII's Mistresses*, Corgi, 1989.

Atkinson, Diane, *Love and Dirt, The Marriage of Arthur Munby & Hannah Cullwick*, Macmillan, 2003.

Boswell, James, *The Journals of James Boswell, 1761–1796*, ed., John Wain, Heinemann, 1990.

Boswell, James, *The Life of Samuel Johnson*, vols 1&2, Odhams Press.

Boswell, James, *London Journal, 1762–1763*, ed., Frederick A. Pottle, Heinemann, 1950.

Burford, E.J., *Bawds & Lodgings*, Peter Owen, 1976.

Burge, James, *Abelard & Heloise*, Harper One, 2006.

Casanova, Giacomo, trans., Willard R. Trask, *The History of My Life*, 12 vols, Longman, 1971.

Chaucer, Geoffrey, *The Canterbury Tales*, Penguin Classics, 2003.

Cruikshank, Dan, *The Secret History of Georgian London*, Random House, 2009.

Dabbhoiwala, Faramerz, *The Origins of Sex, A History of the First Sexual Revolution*, Allen Lane, 2012.

Ellman, Richard, *Oscar Wilde*, Vintage, 1988.

Fabricius, Johannes, *Syphilis in Shakespeare's England*, J. Kingsley, 1994.

Flaubert, Gustave, trans., Francis Steegmuller, *Flaubert in Egypt*, Bodley Head, 1972.

Fraser, Lady Antonia, *Love & Louis XIV: The Women in the Life of the Sun King*, Orion, 2006.

Fraser, Lady Antonia, *King Charles II*, Phoenix, 2002.

Gibbon, Edward, *The Decline & Fall of the Roman Empire*, Wordsworth Editions, 1998.

Gibson, Ian, *The English Vice: Beating, Sex & Shame in Victorian England and After*, Duckworth, 1978.

Herman, Eleanor, *Sex With Kings*, Harper Perennial, 2004.

Latham, Robert, ed., *The Shorter Pepys*, Bell & Hyman, 1985.

Le Roy Ladurie, Emmanuel, trans., Barbara Bray, *Montaillou: The Promised Land of Error*, George Braziller, 2008.

Linnane, Fergus, *London the Wicked City*, Robson Books, 2003.

Love, Brenda, *The Encyclopedia of Unusual Sex Practices*, Abacus, 2012.

McKenna, Neil, *Fanny & Stella: The Young Men Who Shocked Victorian England*, Faber, 2013.

Mitford, Nancy, *Madame de Pompadour*, Vintage Classics, 2011.

Mitford, Nancy, *The Sun King*, Vintage Classics, 2011.

Norwich, John Julius, *Absolute Monarchs: A History of the Papacy*, Random House, 2012.

Paoli, Ugo Enrico, *Rome, Its People, Life & Customs*, Bristol Classical Press, 1992.

Parissien, Steven, *George IV*, St Martin's Press, 2001.

Parker, Geoffrey, *At the Court of the Borgia*, Folio Society, 1963.

Picard, Liza, *Dr Johnson's London*, Weidenfeld & Nicolson, 2000.

Picard, Liza, *Elizabeth's London: Everyday Life in Elizabethan London*, Weidenfeld & Nicolson, 2003.

Picard, Liza, *Restoration London: Everyday Life in the 1660s*, Phoenix, 2004.

Potter, D. S. and D. J. Mattingly, eds, *Life, Death & Entertainment in the Roman Empire*, University of Michigan, 1999.

Roberts, Andrew, *Napoleon & Wellington: The Long Duel*, Phoenix, 2003.

Roberts, Nickie, *Whores in History, Prostitution in Western Society*, Harper Collins, 1993.

Rochester, John Wilmot, Earl of, *The Complete Poems*, ed. David M. Vieth, Routledge & Keegan Paul, 1953.

Rubenhold, Hallie, ed., *Harris' List*, Transworld Publishers, 2012.

Shelton, Jo-Ann, *As the Romans Did*, Oxford University Press, 1988.

Tannahill, Reay, *Sex in History*, Sphere Books Ltd, 1989.

Tomalin, Claire, *Samuel Pepys: The Unequalled Self*, Viking, 2002.

Quennell, Peter, *London's Underworld: Being Selections from Henry Mayhew*, Spring Books, 1950.

Waller, Maureen, *1700: Scenes from London Life*, Sceptre, 2001.

Weir, Alison, *The Six Wives of Henry VIII*, Vintage, 2007.

Weis, René, *The Yellow Cross – the Story of the Last Cathars 1290–1329*, Penguin, 2001.

Wilson, Mary, *Venus Schoolmistress*, 1877.

Zacks, Richard, *History Laid Bare, Love, Sex & Perversity from the Ancient Etruscans to Lawrence of Arabia*, Michael O'Mara Books, 1995.

Websites:
http://www.medievalists.net
http://www.ocp.hul.harvard.edu/contagion/syphilis
http://victorianlondon.org

ACKNOWLEDGEMENTS

I would particularly like to thank Diane Atkinson for introducing me to the strange but fascinating world of Hannah and Arthur, and my husband Trevor, whose lifelong interest in Johnson, Boswell, and their London life was the starting point for many stories. Finally to everyone at Michael O'Mara, especially Louise Dixon for commissioning me to write this book: it's been an education.

PICTURE ACKNOWLEDGEMENTS

LUCRETIUS: Picture courtesy of the Thomas Fisher Rare Book Library, University of Toronto

PRIAPUS: Clipart.com

NERO: IStockphoto.com

COCK LANE: Ted West / Central Press / Getty Images

CHASTITY BELT (either pic): Clipart.com

ULRICH VON LIECHTENSTEIN: Prisma / UIG / Getty images

FLAGELLANTS: Clipart.com

MADAM DE POMPADOUR: Frontispiece from *Madame la Marquise de Pompadour* by M. Capefigue, 1860, based on a painting by Maurice Quentin de la Tour, 1755 (shown in the Louvre museum, Paris)

CATHERINE THE GREAT: Popperfoto / Getty Images

TATTOO (warriors): Hulton Archive / Getty Images

BAGNIO: Library of Congress (LC-USZ62-132976)

INDEX

INDEX

Hippocrates 13–14, 44, 206
Hogarth, William 153–4
Hogg, Thomas 134
homosexuality
  Ancient Greece 11, 12
  Egypt 198–9
  Ernest Boulton and Frederick Park 173–5
  medieval period 38
  molly houses 168–9
  Oscar Wilde 175–8
  Renaissance Italy 54
  Roman 21–2, 23, 31–2
  Sir Richard Burton 200
  William Bankes 172
Hooker, General Joseph 157
Howard, Catherine 92

I
incest 33, 38, 73, 74, 84, 90, 139
Innocent IV, Pope 67
Inquisitions 59, 63, 65–70
Isabella I of Castile 68
Isabella II of Spain 68

J
John V of Portugal, King 123
Johnson, Samuel 129, 187–8
Josephine, Empress 192–5
Julius II, Pope 75–6

K
Kama Shastra Society 201
Kama Sutra 201
Keller, Rose 130–1
Kérouaille, Louise de 104, 105, 106–7, 118
King, Tom and Moll 159–60
Kotzwara, Franz 137

L
Lamb, Lady Caroline 138–9
Larkin, Philip 7
Launay, Anne-Prospère de
Leczinska, Marie 115

Lennard, Anne (Countess of Sussex) 109, 110
lesbianism 14, 108, 109, 171–2
Liechtenstein, Ulrich von 50–1
Lloyd, Constance 176
Louis IX of France, King 38
Louis XIV of France, King 106, 111–13, 118
Louis XV of France, King 115–19
Lucretius 17
Ludwig I of Bavaria, King 122
Luther, Martin 77–9

M
Madame Bovary (G. Flaubert) 199
madams *see* bawds/madams; brothels; prostitution
Mailly-Nesle, Louise-Julie de 115
Maintenon, Madame de 111, 114
Mancini, Hortense 107–10, 115
Marie of Champagne 49
Mark Anthony 28
marriage 9–10, 13, 16, 17, 19–20, 43, 44, 45, 46, 48, 69, 77–9
  see also adultery
Martial 22
Marx, Karl 196
Mary I, Queen 95
Massagatae tribe 16
masturbation 14, 122, 204–7
Medici, Catherine de 98–9
Medmenham Abbey, Marlowe 135
Meibom, Johann Heinrich 145–6
Milbanke, Anne Isabella 138–9
molly houses 168–9
Mons, Anna 125

Montagu, Lady Mary Wortley 196–7
Montaillou, France 63–5
Montespan, Françoise Athénaïs de 111, 112–14
Montez, Lola 122
Monvoisin, Catherine 'La Voisin' 112–13
Mother Clap's molly house 169–70
Munby, Arthur 208–15

N
Napoleon Bonaparte, Emperor 192–5
Napoleon III, Emperor 125–6
Needham, Elizabeth 'Mother' 153–4, 167
Nero, Emperor 34–5
Nicomedes IV of Bithynia, King 23
Nocturnal Night Revels (Anon.) 155–6

O
Obscene Publications Act (1857) 143, 201
Of Plymouth Plantation (W. Bradford) 133–4
orgies 32, 75, 124, 131

P
Parc-aux-Cerfs, Versailles 117
Park, Frederick 173–5
pederasty 12, 200–1
Pepys, Samuel 100, 104, 150, 180–2
Perfumed Garden (trans. Sir R. Burton) 201
Peter the Great 125
piercings 23, 140
pimps 41, 151–2
Pinto, Dr Pedro 81
Pius II, Pope 71
plague 48, 79
Planissoles, Béatrice de 64, 65–6
Plato 12
Pliny the Elder 19, 29, 31
Plutarch 30

INDEX

Pool Hall Chairs

Noah Hawley
"Before The Fall"

John Grisham (New)
"Camino Island"